No Tears

No Tears

MY JOURNEY FROM BEING A WAR CHILD IN AFRICA TO A FOSTER CHILD IN AMERICA

Christiana Crawley

Christiana F Crawley

ISBN: 1517042402
ISBN 13: 9781517042400
Library of Congress Control Number: 2015914885
CreateSpace Independent Publishing Platform
North Charleston, South Carolina

Prologue

SOMETIMES WHEN I CLOSE MY eyes I can still see them. I can hear the terrified screams of men as they are chopped to pieces in front of their own children. I can still see the blood pooling on the ground beneath the bodies of the dead and dying. I can hear the sobs of children kneeling over the bodies of their fallen parents.

The things I saw and the suffering I have witnessed will never be erased from my mind. Even after all of these years, I still jump every time I hear a firework. I hate fireworks. I still wake up at night wondering if I am safe. I check the locks throughout the day. I wonder if I will ever feel safe.

After suffering through war, near slavery, and rape, I am finally safe. But the truth is I will never feel that way. Some wounds are too deep to heal; some scars will never fade, no matter how much time has passed. After what I have been through, it is a miracle I have escaped as safely as I have. I am just so grateful that God has carried me through it all, and protected me every step of the way.

CHAPTER 1

Happy Beginnings

I WAS VERY YOUNG WHEN the war reached our part of Sierra Leone. I only have a few memories of life before the war. My father was a police officer. We lived in the barracks with all of the other police officers' families in Grafton Freetown. The homes were close together and separated by a small dirt road.

My earliest memory was when I was very little, barely able to walk. I hated eating. I do not know why, but I just did not like it. The only thing I wanted to eat was breast milk. My mom tried to give me some baby formula every now and then, but every time I finished drinking it, I would crawl away on the cement floor of our home, and throw it up. I did it so much that my grandma made up a song to help me keep my formula down. The song did not work; I still would not eat anything.

My mom would give me a little purple bowl full of rice every day. I would smile really big and go out the front door and across the little dirt road holding the bowl with both hands. My friend, Emmanuel, lived in the home right across from ours. I walked across the road and knocked on Emmanuel's door. His mom opened it up and let me in. I handed Emmanuel my bowl and he ate all of the rice. After he finished, I took back the empty bowl and walked home and gave it to my mother.

"Did you eat it?" she asked. I nodded my head excitedly. She frowned, "No you didn't. I remember this would happen every day.

In the barracks, I shared a room with my two aunts, my sisters Miatta and Messie, and my grandma. My grandma had her own little bed, but the rest of us all shared a bed. We used to lay every which way all over each other. I slept on that same mattress during my entire childhood. It stunk horribly and was covered in bedbugs. Every morning I would wake up scratching. Some other extended family members slept in the family room, and my parents had their own room.

When my Dad was home he would gather us all together in the family room every night and he would stand and pray for us, and bless us. I remember him thanking God for all that we had, and asking him to bless each of us by name. I could feel the faith that he had, and I knew that someone was listening to those prayers.

We had a little dirt patio in front of our house that I used to love playing on. My mom said that when I was about 14 months old, our neighbor would come by after work while I was playing out there. He would say "one-eighty" and I would do the splits all the way down to the ground and he would give me candy.

Off to the side of our patio, my cousin set up a tarp that hung over the front of our porch. He did this so we had somewhere to keep the monkeys tied up that he caught for food.

One day, I was sitting out there with the monkeys. For some reason I was eating handfuls of dirt. Apparently it tasted better than the formula my mom was always trying to feed me. My dad came through the fence in the front yard and saw me eating dirt.

"What are you doing?" he yelled, and picked me up by my arm and spanked me with two fingers. It did not hurt, but I was so surprised that I cried and cried.

It makes me smile to think about being that little girl. I did not have any worries. The worst thing I had ever experienced was a little spank from my dad. In Africa, parents would hit their kids when they misbehaved, but with my parents it was never excessive. They loved me, and took care of me. They protected me during the worst moments of my early life.

My next memory was in nursery school. My cousin Foday made me a little desk that I could sit in while I did my work. It was made out of wood, and it was one of the only possessions I had. I was so happy to have it, and I was so proud of it. School was a couple of blocks away. I remember I would carry my desk to school and sit in it proudly throughout the school day.

At the end of school, I would take it home with me. "You do not need to take it home every day Feima" my mom would say, (she always called me by my middle name) but I did not listen. I wanted to bring it home because I did not want anybody else sitting in it while I was gone.

It was the most valuable thing I owned. I wanted to protect it. It is amazing to think that having just one thing of my own made me so happy. Sometimes when I look at the things kids have in the United States and how they act I wonder if we would all be happier with less.

All of these memories were very happy. I felt so safe. I felt so happy. I had my mom there to protect me, and to love me. I was surrounded by my family and friends. We were poor, but I had everything a little girl needed. My dad was away in the city for weeks at a time working, but when he was home we were all together and life was perfect.

During those years I do not have many memories, I remember feelings more than events. I just remember feeling happy. I remember being worry free and having fun every day.

CHAPTER 2

The War Begins

EVENTUALLY, I TURNED FOUR YEARS old and finished nursery school. It was the day of my nursery school graduation; it was a day that will forever be etched into my memory. My mom gave me a bath in front of our house. She bathed me quickly because the water was so cold. She washed my hair, and then dried me off and helped me put my underwear on, and then went inside to get my clothes

When she came back out I did not want to get the rest of the way dressed. I should have been so excited to go to my graduation, but I was not. I just ran around in front of our house and played.

Across the street, my friend Emmanuel got bathed and was having his head shaved. He was so excited to graduate.

"Look at Emmanuel. Look at him get ready to go. Don't you want to get ready?" my mom asked.

"No," I said with a shrug and just kept playing in the yard. Right at that moment we started hearing gunshots.

"It sounds like the soldiers are practicing," my mom said as she walked back into the house. The soldiers practiced frequently so I did not really think anything of it. I kept playing in the yard, waiting for my mom to give up on making me go to school. The sound of gunshots continued and started to get more frequent. My mom kept on opening the front door and looking toward the shots.

She was standing on the front porch and I was playing a few feet away from her when suddenly we heard a loud boom, followed by another. The sound of the bombs was so loud I felt like it was making my skin vibrate. There was a slight breeze coming from where the gunshots were, and I could smell smoke in the air.

"Get in the house Feima!" my mom yelled as she ran into the yard. She grabbed my hand and we ran up the stairs and into the house. Once we were both inside, with the rest of our family, she locked the door and closed all of the windows. I did not know what was going on, but I was starting to get scared. Why was she acting this way? There was intensity in her eyes that I had never seen before. My father came in from his bedroom and they started whispering to each other. They were standing so rigidly. We just waited like this for two hours.

A knock came at our door and a man came in. "The war is here" he said. After he came in, more and more people started coming into our house to hide. Emmanuel and his parents were both there with us. Emmanuel and I did not say anything; we just stood by our parents quietly.

After people stopped coming into the house, my mom locked the door again. The man that came and told us about the war told everybody to get underneath the beds. I slid underneath the bed on my stomach in between my sisters. We laid there in silence. I did not say anything to anybody. We just listened to the gunshots and bombs going off in the distance.

Everyone was breathing really heavily. Even though it was past midnight, none of us were even close to falling asleep. Slowly, the gunshots started to get louder until finally we started to hear bullets hitting the walls in our house. I wanted to scream, but I remembered the adults told us all not to make a sound or they might find us and kill us.

So we just waited, terrified about what might happen next. I do not remember how long this continued, but it felt like a really long time. I guess the soldiers were just walking through the city shooting all of the houses figuring they would kill more people if they just shot into all of the windows and walls as they walked by. Thankfully, nobody came inside. They probably saw that all of the other homes were empty and thought everybody had fled.

When it finally got quiet, my dad got up and silently peaked out the window. "They are gone," he said. We waited a little while to make sure they did not come back. We then gathered what food we had and some extra clothes, wrapping them in a cloth, and left.

My dad led the way out the back door. We snuck through our backyard as noiselessly as possible, and made our way into the jungle. It was very dark outside. As I walked through the jungle, there was a unique fragrance of smoke mixed with the green smell of the forest.

Once we were a little ways away from the house, we decided it was safe to make a little more noise and so we started to run. It was so cold. The wet leaves kept hitting my face as I followed after my dad. Before long I was soaking wet from sweat and the wet leaves brushing against me. My clothes stuck to my skin tightly as if I had just walked out of a pond fully clothed. The ground was covered in mud, and eventually we were too.

We kept going until my legs were too tired to keep moving. They ached so much. We wanted to stop, but whenever we were tempted to stop we heard more gunshots and knew that we had to keep going. We had to get away. As we traveled many of the people broke away from the group to go looking for their families.

The jungle did not go on for miles; every now and then we would have to cross a street or at least get close to one. After crossing one of the streets, we heard yelling followed by gunshots. I am not sure, but I think they were shooting at us.

After a while we came to a huge river. Tired and weak, everyone began to swim across. I could not swim well enough to cross a river like this, even during the day, but with how exhausted I was, it was not even a possibility. I climbed on Foday's back and he approached the river.

As he walked down into the water and my legs dipped into it, I immediately was hit by the cold. The water was so freezing. I gasped as he lowered himself into the water and started swimming on his stomach. I tried to keep my head above the water, but my face kept on dipping into it as Foday tried his best to swim with me on his back. By the time we got to the other side I was shivering uncontrollably.

After I climbed down from his back, we did not hesitate at all. My dad immediately began to run again. I warmed up a little as we continued to run. About 20 minutes later we came to a large hill. It was too dark to really tell how high it went, but my Dad seemed to know where he was going. I looked up at the hill with despair. I was so tired. *How can I climb a hill when I am this tired?* I thought.

I was really scared, I did not know what was going on, so I just followed everyone. The climb was agonizing. Several times I felt like I was going to collapse from exhaustion. Finally we came upon a house. I could tell there was a candle burning inside, by the flickering I could see through the window. My dad knocked on the door, and a man I did not recognize answered and let us in. My dad spoke quietly with him for a few minutes and then turned to us and said, "We are staying here tonight."

I collapsed on one of the beds with my two sisters and closed my eyes. I had never been pushed so hard, or been so horrified. The combination of fear and fatigue took over and I started to fall asleep immediately. As I drifted off, I remember hearing my parents talk with the other adults. They were trying to decide where to go next.

As I woke up the next morning, before I opened my eyes, I thought maybe it was all a dream. Maybe I will open my eyes and be in my own bed at home. I was sad to open them and see I was in a strange place. The war was real, and there was no way I could escape my new reality.

I went in the other room where the adults had been talking the night before, and my parents were not in there. I looked around the house and they were not in any of the rooms. I was so terrified. I did not know where they were!

I started to cry frantically. I felt so afraid of what had happened to my life, and wondered if I would ever see them again. One of the women we were staying with approached me. "Do not be afraid child," she said as she crouched down next to me. "Your parents have gone to Freetown to find a safe place for us all to go."

I waited there all morning, wondering what was to become of me. I imagined all of the worst things that could have happened. I worried that the men we were running from may have caught them. That afternoon as I sat quietly in the main area of the small house, a knock came at the door and my father walked in followed by my mother. I was so happy to see them. I sprang forward and buried my face in my mother's dress and cried.

"Please do not leave again," I said through my tears.

"We are going to stay together from now on," she said.

For some reason, Emmanuel and his family decided not to go with us to Freetown. Because everybody was in such a hurry, I did not really get the chance to say goodbye to Emmanuel or his family. We were rushed away it seemed in an instant and back to running, and hiding.

My memory is somewhat vague from this point until we reached Freetown, but I remember when we got to Freetown we arrived at a huge house. It was my Uncle Augastine's house. It was the biggest house I had ever seen. It had two stories and plenty of bedrooms. We decided it would be safer to split into smaller groups, so my grandma, sisters, and my cousin would stay at this house and my parents and I would go to my other uncle, Uncle James's house to hide.

We all gave each other hugs, and said goodbye. I was still so confused. I did not realize that this might be the last time I saw my sisters, my grandma, and Foday. After walking another couple of miles we arrived at my Uncle James's house. It was much smaller and only had two bedrooms.

When Uncle James came to the door and saw us, he welcomed us in and had us sit down. There were other families there that were obviously hiding like we were, but he welcomed us anyway. He brought us some dried fruit he had in his storage. We soaked some Gari (dried cassava roots) he had with water and ate it like oatmeal.

After we finished eating, the adults sent all of the kids into one of the bedrooms so they could discuss things. We were all so scared; we did not play or anything. We just sat there quietly waiting to see what would happen next.

My uncle told us to sleep in his bedroom. We had to stay under the bed all day because we did not want the rebels to know anybody was home. We could not eat or go outside to go to the bathroom. Only at night, could we come out, but we could not light any lamps. We just had to go off of the little light that the moon and stars provided as they shone in through the windows. Because it was dark outside, I was allowed to sleep on top of the bed. I do not remember my parents ever sleeping during the war.

Thankfully either by luck or by our caution the rebels did not find us.

CHAPTER 3

Horrific Violence of War

I DO NOT KNOW HOW long we stayed at Uncle James's house, but it seemed like a long time. One night we heard shouting outside. We came out into the family room and crouched down and peeked out the windows. We had to be very careful because if the rebels saw any movement they would come in and kill everybody.

I remember carefully peeking out the window next to my dad. There was a huge house across the street from us. There were many families staying in it, including several pregnant women and several nursing mothers. The rebels must have heard the babies crying, because somehow they found out that people were hiding there.

While we were looking out the window, all of a sudden we heard noises. Rebels came out and filled the street. They were carrying torches, and yelling loudly. "We know you are in there!" one of them yelled.

Some of the rebels came forward and used their torches to set the house on fire. They then surrounded the house, and continued to light it on fire in different places. The rebels continued to light smaller objects on fire and proceeded to throw them through the windows of the house. As the fire started to engulf the house, the screams started. I watched as a woman tried to run out of the house. She jumped off of the porch and tried to sprint away from the house, but before she could get away she was shot down by several of the rebels.

I could not believe what I had just seen. They killed her! There were people dying in that house. I could hear them screaming as their bodies burned--as their children burned. I knew I was not supposed to make any sound so I did not cry out loud, but that did not stop tears from rolling down my cheeks.

As others tried to escape they were killed as well. We all watched, stunned and terrified, as men and women were shot down, their bodies collecting on the ground outside of the house riddled with bullets. We listened to the agonizing screams of men, women, and little children burning to death in the house. Some of them came running out of the burning house, and as their skin burned and melted off of their bodies, they were shot to death.

This continued until the screaming subsided. The rebels waited outside of the house and watched it burn to make sure there were no survivors. We were all so paralyzed with shock that we did not realize the danger we had put ourselves in by being out of our hiding place for so long. My dad motioned for us to follow him back into the bedroom. I quietly followed them into the room and slid back underneath the bed between my parents.

As I laid there on the uncomfortable cement floor, what I had just seen finally started to settle in. I cried quietly as I wondered if I was going to be lit on fire. I started to have an awful feeling that my mom or dad would be one of those people, covered in blood, lying on the ground full of bullets.

By this time it was almost light outside. I laid there and tried to fall asleep, but every time I closed my eyes I would see the victims. I could not stop hearing their screams. These were the men we were running from. Finally, after just following my parents and doing what they said, I realized why we were doing it. We were running away from pure evil.

Eventually, we ran out of food. At night we would sneak out and find fruit. We would bring it back and slice it up and share it. Then we would lay under the bed again for a full day, hungry and tired. The worst part was that we had to wait until night-time to use the bathroom, which would have been a lot worse if we had enough to eat or drink. The harsh truth was that we really did not eat or drink enough to have any accidents.

One day, the rebels gathered out in the streets. One of them shouted into a mega-phone: "OK, COME OUT AND WE WILL LET YOU GO, IF YOU WEAR OR HOLD SOMETHING WHITE AND SING WHILE YOU WALK AWAY!"

For some reason we believed them. It might have been because we knew we were trapped and it was only a matter of time before they found us. There were only so many houses they needed to check. Whatever the reason, we all gathered anything we could find that was white, and put it on or held it.

We came out and started walking down the middle of the road. We were singing the song that they told us to sing, and waving our white objects and clothing in the air. People were starting to come out from other buildings and eventually it seemed like they were really going to let us go. It almost felt like a celebration. I waved my white cloth above my head as I sang.

Suddenly, we heard gunfire. My dad grabbed my arm and we ran as fast as we could back into the house. My mom and I quickly crawled under the bed, and my dad parted the drapes just enough to see down into the street. "They are killing everybody," he said. "Stay under the bed!"

During the following days, the rebels continued to try and trick people. My dad told us that they all seemed to be stumbling around like they were high or drunk. I am guessing the reason they kept trying to trick people to come out is because they were too lazy to search every house, or too high to do it in an organized way.

One of the ways they tricked a few people is by ringing the church bell in one of the mosques. Somehow people thought that this meant that the rebels had left and that we were all going to the church to pray. I was told that when those people went into the mosque, the rebels would jump out from hiding and throw bombs at them and blow them up.

We kept on surviving this way, hiding during the day, scavenging for food at night. Eventually my uncle realized that the rebels were not leaving anytime soon. He needed to go get his daughter back from where she was hiding so that they could be together. He left at about 2:00 A.M. to go find her.

A few hours later we heard somebody yell "HALT!" I froze as the hair on my arms and neck stood up. I flinched as gunshots roared right outside of the house. After about 30 seconds the gunshots ended.

We were too scared to go to the door to see what happened. We did not want to even move for fear that they would hear us and light the house on fire. After about an hour, my parents went and slowly opened the door. They found my uncle laying there in a puddle of blood. He and his little girl were both dead. He was lying on his side covered in bullet holes, his two year old daughter wrapped in his arms. His eyes were wide open, staring into space. Hers were closed.

After this happened we knew we had to keep moving, so we immediately left. All we took with us was a small bundle of extra clothes and a little bit of fruit we had gathered. I was running behind my parents and the rebels were camped out not too far behind us. One of them saw us running and yelled, "Halt!"

We kept running and they yelled, "Halt or we will shoot!"

My dad paused. We stood still as they walked toward us. I looked back at them and was surprised to see that both of them were very young, probably teenagers. Suddenly, my dad yelled, "Run!" He bolted forward. "Run as fast as you can! They will miss us!"

So we ran. We ran as fast as we could as bullets whipped past us in the air. We came to a barbed wire fence and quickly shuffled underneath it. As my mom slid underneath, her eyebrow got caught on a barb and was sliced in half. Because we ran fast and probably because they were so high, they never caught up with us. I am so grateful that my father decided to run. There is no way they would have let us live if they caught us, and they would probably have killed us in very painful ways.

As we ran, we passed dozens of dead bodies. I felt myself getting sick as the smell of death became stronger. There was so much blood on the ground. Mixed in with the dirt it did not even look red--it was more of a dark brown. I was so shocked, I felt numb. I jumped to the side as I almost stepped in a puddle of blood.

As we ran we came across a woman who was lying in the middle of the road. She was covered in blood. Her arms, lower legs, and breasts were all cut off. Her stomach was sliced open and her unborn baby was lying dead next to her discarded limbs. The rebels played a game with pregnant women. They would ask, "Do you think it's a boy or a girl?" Then they would say, "Let's find out." Then, the rebels would slice open your stomach and make you watch your baby die as they chopped you up.

"Please" she coughed out, as blood trickled down the corner of her mouth. "Please save my baby," she begged, her eyes pleading with us more than her words. My mom stood there with her hand over her mouth. None of us knew what to say. She died while we were standing over her. Her eyes frozen open with that same pleading look. We knew the rebels were close, they must have just finished doing this to her, because she could not have survived for long like that, so we kept moving.

As we ran we spotted some people that were hiding in a bush. There was a little puddle of water there and none of us had taken a drink in a long time, so we crouched down and drank the muddy water. It was warm and I could feel the flecks of dirt roll down my throat with the water, but I was so thirsty I drank it greedily. It was starting to get dark and we had not heard any rebels or gunshots for about an hour.

There was a burnt structure there that just had walls and no roof. "We will sleep here tonight," my dad said. I sat down and leaned my head on my mother's shoulder. There was an old man sitting across from me on the other side of the burnt structure. Something did not look right about him.

He looked back at me with an empty look in his eyes. It seemed as if he was deflated, like he was completely out of life. I fell asleep there leaning on my mom. When I woke up in the morning the old man was still sitting across from me, but he was not moving. My dad went and checked on him.

"He is not breathing...He is dead," my dad said.

We all took a long drink from the muddy puddle and set out again. We traveled at a more relaxed pace that day. I guess my dad somehow knew that we were not in immediate danger anymore. After the things I had seen, I would have been fine running again if he wanted to, but we all were very hungry and thirsty so walking was probably a good idea.

Finally we arrived at the entrance to the refugee camp in Bai-Bureh Road. There was a huge line of people trying to get in. We were really happy to see my cousin, sisters and grandma all in the line. It had only been a few weeks since we last saw each other, but it felt like a lifetime. We got in line about 40 people behind them. Foday waved at me and smiled. I smiled back happily. Foday lived in my house with me my whole life. He was more of a brother than a cousin.

Our happy waves and smiles were interrupted by some kind of disturbance going on in the line. They had stopped letting people into the city. A soldier was standing by the entrance with a woman by his side. Her hands were tied together. She was obviously a prisoner.

"This woman is a rebel. She will be telling us who among you are rebels in exchange for her life!" the soldier yelled as he held her by the back of her neck.

"They are making sure no rebels get into the city," my mother whispered to me.

The woman stepped forward and pointed at a man. "He helped me kill many people," she said. The soldiers grabbed him by the neck and pulled him out of the line.

"I am not a rebel! She is lying!" he screamed. "I am not a rebel!" The soldier cut him off by chopping down hard on his right arm with a sharp machete. It sliced through skin and bone. The man fell to the earth convulsing and screaming. The soldier grabbed him by his other arm. He placed his boot against the man's chest and pulled his arm tight. He hacked off this arm with two strokes of the machete.

"Let's see you shoot us with no arms rebel!" the soldier yelled at him.

My mother tried to pull me behind her so I would not see, but I could not look away. I could not get myself to stop watching. They moved down the line. The woman pointed out another man. The soldier grabbed him by his hair and slit his throat. The blood poured out as he gurgled and convulsed on the ground. The crowd started to sense that these men were not really rebels and none of us were safe. They skipped a few women and children and moved on to the next man. Again the woman claimed he was a rebel, and again his blood was spilt.

My eyes will never be healed from the terror they saw that day. Men begging for their lives, terror frozen in their eyes as their arms or legs were chopped from their bodies, blood pooling on the ground in gallons, women screaming, children crying next to the corpses of their bloodied fathers and brothers. Some of them died quickly, but there were several that were screaming in agony, bleeding to death slowly.

Some they would chop off their hands or arms, others they would slit their throats, and some they would just stab through the heart or shoot in the head. Blood and tears, screaming and death, widowed mothers and fatherless children covered in the blood of their dying and dead loved ones, kneeling in agony at the feet of our own soldiers.

My shock was broken and replaced with utter terror as I realized my cousin was only a few people ahead in the line. I felt my heart drop into my stomach. Of course he was not a rebel, but that did not matter. This woman was lying in order to kill more of us. I started to cry out, and my mother grabbed me and held my mouth shut. Tears sprang from my eyes as I watched the men chop off the legs of a man three people away from Foday. I buried my face in my mother's leg, not wanting to see my Cousin die.

Suddenly, I felt her relax. I peeked ahead at Foday. He was fine. The soldiers were a few feet away. Somehow they had found out that the woman was lying. They threw her to the ground and unceremoniously shot her in the head. Her body slumped to the ground, the only justified killing that day.

The soldiers then let all of us into the city. I stared at the ground as we walked past the soldiers. I was just as scared of them as I was of the rebels.

I do not know what happened to the men that were still alive--the ones that had lost limbs. I can only imagine the bitterness they must feel. The betrayal they must have felt, as those they looked to for protection butchered and maimed them.

CHAPTER 4

Recovering From War

THERE WAS NOT ENOUGH ROOM for everybody in normal housing so the soldiers put us in a huge warehouse. There were so many people in there and even more mosquitoes. It was so hot and so itchy; my skin was constantly covered in sweat. It seemed like no matter how hard I tried not to, I was always bumping into someone. For some reason we were not allowed to leave, so people were going to the bathroom right there in the room. I could not get over the stench. It smelled like sweat and urine. I could feel so many people breathing. It was very nauseating.

The first day that we were there the soldiers brought us a few cans of peas. We were so hungry; they tasted like the most amazing thing in the world. The problem was that that was all they continued to give us, just peas and water. I guess that is all they had.

Luckily, towards the end, the food got better. The soldiers brought us some really dry food bars. We ground them up and mixed them with water and made a kind of cereal.

I do not remember how long we stayed in the warehouse, but I do remember that we finally were able to feel safe. And as soon as it was safe to return to Grafton, we traveled home.

I do not really remember traveling back home, I think the only reason I remember any of the other things is because they were so scary.

After we got back to Grafton, I started school again. The school I went to was called

"Freetown Teachers College Practicing School". The war was still going on in other places, but things were back to normal in Grafton.

My first day in first grade I was so scared to be left alone so far away from home, so I made my mom come with me and stand in the back of the class. Every now and then I would look back at her, she would smile at me and I would feel safe again. I started looking back less and less and eventually she stopped coming.

Life continued and I progressed into the 2nd and then the 3rd grade. When I was in the 3rd grade I went to go visit my mom at the college during lunch. When I got back, everybody in the school was talking and laughing. They all were carrying around these cute little dolls and other interesting looking items.

"Where did you get that?" I asked a little girl in my class.

"Some white people came and brought them," she said excitedly. "Didn't you get one?"

"No…. Are there any more?" I asked, tears welling up in my eyes.

"No they gave one to everybody and then they took the rest with them," she said.

I felt a lump forming in my throat as I watched everybody play with the dolls that came in the care packages. They all had new toothbrushes, toothpaste, a first aid kit, and a beautiful brand new doll. Every doll I had ever owned was ratty and old. I could hardly contain my tears. After school was over I ran home and cried to my mom. I told her the whole story, and then buried my head in her lap and cried some more. I was probably crying for over an hour.

"Messie come in here please" my mom said. "I need you to share your doll and first aid kit with Feima, okay?"

Messie was not very happy about it, but she agreed to share and I calmed down. It probably sounds pretty silly how heartbroken I was, but in Africa owning a new toy was so rare. So rare, in fact, that because I missed that chance I never did own a new toy of my own.

Other than that, my life was very happy. I went to school, played, spent time with my mom and grandma, and time moved swiftly. During my 5th grade year I was sick often. I had yellow fever, malaria and whatever else the mosquitoes drug in. In the United States when people hear about malaria, they think it is some kind of terrifying illness. While it is scary, the truth is when you have something so often it just does not scare you anymore.

Whenever I came down with malaria, my mom would lay me down on my grandma's mat and check my temperature with her hand. Sometimes, if we could afford it, she would buy me some pain medication, and then she would get the bark from a mango tree and boil it. After it was extremely hot she would put the boiling pot on the ground next to a stool. Then I would sit on the stool and she would put a really heavy blanket over my whole body--including my head--and have the outside of the blanket drape over the pot of boiling mango bark.

I would just sit there and sweat and sweat. Eventually really gross stuff started to ooze out of my skin and the sickness would start to fade. I had malaria so often it seemed like I was doing that all of the time during the 5th grade. It was a feeling that is hard to describe, almost like sweating something thicker than sweat, like cream. Most of the time it worked, but sometimes we would need to go see a nurse so she could give me a shot.

Sadly after missing so much school I had bad news coming up. At the end of the school year, everybody went to the school and stood in line to get their final report cards. My mom and I stood in line. I watched as all of the children excitedly showed their report cards to each other and to their parents. When I was handed mine, I was shocked and devastated to see that I had failed.

I cried and cried and cried. On our way home my mom bought me some treats, but it did not help. I could not stop thinking about how all of my friends would be in a different grade than me. I could not stop thinking of what my dad would say. He was going to be so ashamed of me. He would probably yell at me.

When we arrived back at the police barracks, everybody was showing off their report cards and running around. I ran inside and cried to my grandma. I stayed in that whole day and did not go and play, because all anybody wanted to talk about was their report card. My mom eventually told everybody inside of our house to stop being so excited, to just calm down, and talk about something else

I did not want my dad to find out and be mad at me. That night he called and my mom explained everything to him, and why it was not my fault. When he came home later that month he told me it was okay and that he knew I would do better next year. My mom was always looking out for me. It was how she always took care of me, and protected me that I would miss the most.

CHAPTER 5

Life in Africa

AFTER THE WAR MY AVERAGE day in Grafton went like this: I would wake up in the morning and sweep the porch. My sister and I would then go and fetch water. Sometimes we would get it at the well and sometimes we would get it at the river. After we carried the buckets of water back on our heads, we would usually take a quick cold shower with some of the water we had just fetched. Then, we would walk to school.

After school I would play with my friends. One of the girls in the neighborhood had a little baby gorilla. Whenever he would see me, he would run up to me and climb up into my arms. I loved walking around holding him on my hip like I would a child.

It was cool that she had a pet. Every animal we had was for food. My cousin Foday used to catch monkeys for us to eat. Most of the time his traps would catch adult monkeys, but sometimes he would catch a baby monkey. When he did, we would raise them under the tarp hung in front of our house until they were big enough to eat or sell.

One day I thought it would be funny to wrap one of the smaller monkeys up in a blanket like a baby. So I went and got this little cute monkey and untied it. I then wrapped him up in a blanket and started walking around the village.

"Oh, who is that?" a neighbor woman said as she walked towards me smiling. "Let me see this cute little baby," she said as she lifted the blanket away from the monkey's face. "Oh! Why would you do that?! What is wrong with you?!" she yelled. I just laughed and kept walking.

This is so much fun, I thought, as I kept walking around tricking people. I decided to make it a regular activity. I was having so much fun, I did not realize that it was time for dinner until my mom came and found me. She did not think the joke was funny either.

My grandma always sold tobacco to make a little extra money so we could afford food. I always told her "someday I am going to go to America and I will send you enough money that you do not need to sell tobacco anymore." I do not know why I was always telling her that. I think it just made me sad how hard she had to work to make that little bit of extra money.

Dinner was almost always the same. We would eat rice with sauce. Sometimes if we were lucky we would get to have some chicken or monkey with it, but most of the time it was just rice. My sister and I would eat everything they gave us, but my grandma and mom would always save some of their food so that we would have something leftover for breakfast the next day.

When my sister and I went to get water in the morning my mom would heat up the rice from the night before, because we did not have a stove she would cook everything over an open fire outside. After it was heated up that was our breakfast. We usually did not have any lunch so our next meal would be dinner.

My sister once told me that in America, kids eat three meals a day, and each meal is something different. I thought she was lying to me. It makes me sad when I remember how little my mom used to eat, and how skinny she was from saving part of her food for our breakfast. She sacrificed so much so that we could have enough.

Because it was so rare to have any kind of electricity, the only lighting we had on a regular basis was oil lamps. We would have to light them up and carry them around the house with us. When the electricity would come on, everybody would get really excited and go and dance around in the street. When the lights came on you could hear the excitement in the whole neighborhood. It usually only lasted a few hours and then it was back to normal.

When it rained all of the kids in the neighborhood would get naked and run around in the rain. It was like getting a free bath without having to fetch water. While it rained, my mom would have us get every bucket we had and put it out to gather rainwater. After all of the buckets were out catching water she would have us scrub the floor on the porch. It was the only time we could have water all over the porch, because it would be a waste to fetch water just to pour it out on the ground.

I always wanted to help clean, but my sister did not like me to. So I would get in a fight with her and we would pull each other's hair. Once I had some kind of proof that we had been fighting, like a scratch or some other injury, I would run inside and tell my grandma that Messie beat me up. My grandma would yell at her. Then I would play until my mom got home.

When I heard her coming I would start crying again and tell her that Messie beat me up. Then she would go and yell at her too. I do not know why, but I just loved getting her into trouble. I think if she would have let me help her, I would not have been so awful.

During this time, my sisters, parents and I usually went to church on Sunday's. When they would bring the bread around during the sacrament my sister and I would take as much as we could fit in our hands. It was the only time we could eat bread, and we were usually famished. After the meeting we would go up to the front and see if there was any leftover bread. We savored every piece we got.

I also remember my friend Agnes and I used to go around the neighborhood praying for people. We were so excited about religion. In fact, we were *so* excited, it did not matter what religion it was. We would go to whatever church seemed fun. There was this one church that everybody stood up the whole time and would sing and shout and the preacher would get really into the sermon.

I remember after being there for a couple of hours we would get so tired all we wanted to do was lay on the ground. One time I was so tired and I realized that people that were going into religious trances all got to sit down and lay on the ground while they were being possessed by "the Spirit." So I flopped on the ground and rolled my eyes back and started shaking everywhere like I was having a seizure.

I could feel the people around me turning around to look down and see what was happening. I convulsed for about a minute and then I just laid there. I thought to myself *Finally! I am able to rest!* I cracked my eyes open and saw that the people around me were looking down at me.

"What did you see?" a woman asked. "What did you see child?"

I hesitated, not knowing what to say. "I saw...angels?" I said, hoping they would believe me.

"She has seen angels! Praise the Lord!" the woman shouted, and then everybody went back to singing. I just laid there and enjoyed my rest.

We went to this meeting every week. It lasted for hours and hours. Usually we had to leave early because we were so tired of standing there.

One day I was walking home with my friends. I was running away from one of them and I tripped over a tall root. I fell flat on my face. After I rolled over and shook off the initial shock, I looked down at my foot and saw that I had broken the nail on my big toe.

I ran home as fast as I could to show it to my mom. She tried to push it down and wrap it up, but realized it was barely hanging on by a little bit of skin.

"Well I do not think we can save it," she said.

"Will it grow back?" I asked.

"Yes, but it will look weird."

I was so sad. I did not want to have an ugly toe. So I decided to pray for my toe. I wrapped up my toe and prayed as hard as I could all day. I then fasted the next day and continued to pray. I really did not want to have an ugly toenail. I tried to pray the way my Dad did. I tried to pray with faith.

Eventually when I took off the wrapping, I was ecstatic to find that my toenail had completely healed. The event, as simple as it was, strengthened my testimony of God even more. Ever since, I have always referred to that toenail as "my miracle nail."

I never could remember a time that my father was not sick. He used to go into mindless rages and start thrashing around on the ground. His eyes would roll back and he would start acting as if he was blind and did not have any control of his body. We would have to hide in the other room so he would not hurt us.

My family told me that my uncle cursed him with a wicked genie that was haunting and tormenting him. My father said he would always see the genie right before he started going into the attack. Often times he would end up hurting himself or breaking things during the episode.

Because he was sick, he never advanced at work and never got a raise. He has been there for over 20 years now and to this day has never received a raise. At his low position his only substantial pay is our housing in the police barracks, a two-bedroom, no bathroom living space. Even with all of this trials I never once heard him complain. He was always faithful that God would take care of us, and so grateful for the smallest blessings. The way he stayed strong during his trials was a great example to me.

One day my oldest sister Miatta ran away with her boyfriend. They were gone for months and months. When they decided to get married, her boyfriend came back to Grafton to ask for my dad's permission. When my dad saw him he was so mad that he locked him in the prison for the night.

After he calmed down, he let him out and gave him permission to marry Miatta. After they got married they moved to Nigeria and we never saw them again.

CHAPTER 6

My Ticket to America

ONE NIGHT OUR NEIGHBORS, THE Vandis, came over and were talking with my parents in the back yard. They were back there for hours talking and talking. Mr. Vandi was the branch president of the church we attended; he and his wife, Sarah, were old family friends of ours.

I was in the family room of our house playing with Messie when my mom came inside and leaned down next to me.

"Come in the back yard with us for a little while," she said.

I followed her to the backyard where Dominic Vandi and his wife were standing with my dad. They all looked at me and seemed to be unsure of who should say something. I stood there awkwardly wondering what was going on.

"You are going to go to America with the Vandis," my mom suddenly said.

"No!" I cried, "I do not want to!"

"You need to go Feima," she said. "It is your only chance to have a better life. You will also be able to help us have a better life if you are in America."

"I won't go! I do not want to be without you!" I shrieked as I started to cry. "Please do not make me go!"

"We will come back later," Dominic said as he got up to leave. "Just remember the appointment next week."

After the Vandi's left, I continued to cry as I begged my parents to let me stay.

"I will miss you too much. I will never see you again," I said through my tears as my mom hugged me.

"I promise we will see you again Feima," she said as she rocked me in her arms. *Why are they sending me away?* I thought. *Don't they love me anymore? Why do they want me to leave forever?* I continued to sob as I fell asleep in my mother's arms.

I moped around the house every day that week. I did not even know how I felt about my parents. Should I be angry at them? They did want me to have a better life, but there was nothing wrong with my life. I was 11 years old. I did not have a care in the world. The war was over and we had enough food to eat. I was happy.

About nine days after the night that they told me about America, we were set up to meet at the immigration office. Dominic came and picked me up early that morning.

As we walked away from my house I started to get really nervous. I felt like I was not able to breathe normally. I just could not believe what was happening.

"You have to tell them that your name is Victoria Vandi," Dominic said as we walked. "Your birthday is April 11th. If they ask you about your mom, tell them that you do not really remember her. You were lost during the war and I found you. I am your dad." His hand tightened on my arm, "YOUR NAME IS VICTORIA VANDI!" He repeated slowly. "If you mess this up it will ruin everything."

I started to feel sick. What if I did mess it up? What would he do to me? He seemed so intense. What would he do to my family?

"Say it," he said. "Say your name is Victoria Vandi."

"My name is Victoria Vandi," I quietly said.

"Say it again."

"My name is Victoria Vandi," I repeated. "My name is Victoria Vandi."

"Just make sure you do not mess up," he said again. "You cannot imagine how much money and time we have spent setting this up. You need to make sure you do everything I say."

"I will," I said.

"Good," he said as we continued onward. We did not say anything else to each other on the way to the immigration office.

When we arrived at the office, Dominic, Sarah, their children, and I were guided into a room. Once we were all in there, a man came in and started asking Dominic and Sarah a lot of questions. He asked each child for their name and birth date.

"What is your name?" he asked.

I swallowed hard. "Victoria Vandi," I quietly said.

"Is this your father?"

"Yes."

"What is your birth date?"

"April 11, 1992," I said as my heart continued to race. He went on and started asking the same questions to Dominic Jr.

I did it. I was safe for now. As we left the building, Dominic told me that we would have a few more meetings like that one, but next time they might ask more questions. He told me to practice saying the things he had told me. He also told me not to tell anybody about what was going on.

During the next few weeks, life went on as normal. I would fetch water with my sister, play with my friends, and sweep the porch, but in the back of my mind all I could think of was how sad I was that I would never see any of the people I loved again.

Eventually, it was time for our next appointment. Dominic came and picked me up early in the morning again. He insisted on picking me up and taking me to the office. He said if they saw me with anybody but him they would get suspicious and stop us from going to America.

We took transportation to Freetown and went inside of a big building. As we waited in the front office, I saw a big clear tank full of water. Every now and then somebody would come by and put a little cup underneath the spout and water would poor out into the cup. It was the most amazing thing I had ever seen. I wanted to go over and try it, but I did not know if it was for us or if it was only for other people.

We went in and met with another man, and again the meeting went well. After Dominic took me home, I went in the bedroom and cried for the rest of the day. It was getting more and more real. I could not bear the thought of never seeing my mother again. My mom brought me food as I sat by my bed and cried.

"It will be okay, Feima," she said as she brushed her hands through my hair. "God will protect you."

I ate the food and climbed into bed. I knew God would protect me; I was not worried about my safety. I just could not imagine life without my family. I fell asleep as I cried into my soggy pillow.

We continued to have these meeting every three or four weeks. I was always asked the same questions. I told them the same thing every time. Sometimes they would ask me for more details about my life. I always told them the story that Dominic gave me.

Dominic was able to get them to make me a new birth certificate by claiming that mine was lost during the war. My parents did not put me in school that year, because I would likely be leaving to America soon. I think that they did not want me going around in public using a different name than Victoria Vandi either.

So I was stuck at home every day. It was so boring. Everybody was at school. All of my friends were gone all day. My dad was gone to the village and my mom was at work. I usually spent the whole day sitting around feeling sorry for myself.

On the upside, when my sister was home, she started spending more time with me. I think because I was leaving she started to be nicer than normal to me. She would let me tag along with her and go to her old school. I do not know why she liked going there, but I was really happy to be with her.

My parents always tried to be really positive about America. My mom was always telling me nice things about it, and how happy I would be there. My dad was in the village most of the time, but when he was home he was over the top optimistic about it as well. I did not really know what they were talking about, but I still trusted them. They were always looking out for me, why would this time be any different?

One night we were all at home together talking. It was one of the few nights that my dad was home. A knock came at the door. My dad went and let Dominic in.

"We got the letter from immigration," Dominic said as he sat down. "We will be leaving next week."

Everybody started getting really excited. I smiled really big, and tried to act like I was really happy, but inside I was dying. The day had finally come. I was going to leave my parents and everything I knew and was used to.

That week we spent a lot of time getting ready. I was so surprised when my mom came home with a brand new suitcase. It had a little elephant painted on the front of it. I think it was the only brand new thing I owned. She also gave me a new pair of shoes. I gave her a big hug.

"I want you to have new things just like Americans do," she said as she wiped a tear from her eye.

The night before I left, my dad was gone at the village working. I was sitting on my bed crying.

"What is wrong Feima?" my mom asked as she sat down next to me.

"Please let me stay with you," I begged as I fell into her lap. "I can't go. Please don't make me go." I sobbed all night, begging for her to let me stay. She rocked me to sleep as she sang to me, and told me how much she loved me. I had buried my face in her dress so many times. I fell asleep with the comfort of her embrace and the familiar smell of the soap she used to wash her clothes calming me.

"Wake up, Feima," my mom said as she shook me. "It is time to go."

I grabbed my bag and walked out the door next to my mom and grandma. As we walked away from my house, I looked back at that familiar porch. I looked back longingly, wondering if I would ever see it again.

"I made you something very special, Feima," my grandma said as she held up a little brown bag. I could smell something good coming from it. I could not tell what it was, but it definitely was not just rice, like we normally had.

When we got to the airport we found out they would not be boarding for quite a while so we sat down in a little building. I was still tired from crying all night, so I leaned on my mother's shoulder and fell asleep.

"The plane is about to leave! Hurry!" my mom said as she shook me awake.

I got up and grabbed my little suitcase with the elephant on it, and followed her out of the building. She quickly handed me off to Dominic and he rushed me forward.

I looked back at them and felt a nauseating feeling in my stomach. I did not even get to hug anybody or say goodbye. As Dominic rushed me forward, the last view I caught of my mother she had her hand over her mouth and was crying.

Some people helped us board the plane, and directed us towards a row of empty seats. I quickly went into the row so I could claim the window seat.

I wanted the window seat so that I could hopefully see my family through the window and wave at them. But I could not see them. The plane started to roll forward, and I sat back in my seat and started to cry again.

I did not get to give my mom a kiss. I did not get to eat the special food that my grandma made me. I had only been gone for five minutes and already I felt so homesick.

I was so tired after crying the whole night before, and from the trauma of leaving my mother and father behind, that I fell asleep. I could not tell how long I was sleeping, but eventually Sarah's daughter Fatimah, woke me up and told me we were in the Ivory Coast. The plane took off again and I fell back asleep.

I woke up again and just sat there in silence as the plane continued forward. I was starting to feel a little less nauseated, but I still missed my parents. We landed in Atlanta, Georgia. Some people came and offered us some food. None of us took any. It made us nervous that people we did not know were offering us food.

I had to use the bathroom, but did not know what to do. How could I go to the bathroom anytime soon? We were thousands of feet in the air. It finally got to the point that I could not hold it any longer, so I finally stopped one of the women that were serving drinks.

"I need to go to the bathroom" I said as I shook my legs trying to ignore the urge.

"Oh that is fine dear, just go down to the end of the aisle and the bathroom is that little door on the left."

I stood up and hurried toward the door she had pointed at. *A bathroom in the sky* I thought. I opened the door and was so amazed to see the toilet. After I was done, I was enchanted by flushing the toilet. I had never flushed a toilet before. In fact, I had never even seen a real toilet before. I went and sat back down in my seat, wondering what new wonders awaited me in America.

When we got off the plane we were put in a room to wait with a few other immigrant families. Eventually we were taken into a room with a man. He was wearing a uniform and looked really official. He asked us if we were who the passport said we were and took our picture. Then we were taken to the boarding area for our next flight.

They brought us sandwiches. I thought it was the weirdest thing. I had never seen sliced ham, sliced turkey, and sliced cheese. The only cheese we had in Africa was the "Laughing Cow" brand of cheese. We all picked a few things out of the sandwich and threw the rest away.

We boarded Delta Airlines to head to Utah. When it took off it was so shaky. It was a smaller plane than the one we were in before and I think there might have been a storm. I was sure we were going to die, but I fell asleep anyway.

We landed December 13, 2005 in Salt Lake City, Utah. After we got off the plane, we walked down the huge hallway at the airport. I was so amazed by the size of the building. It seemed like the building went on and on. Everything was so new, so different. I felt like I was in a different world.

Eventually we came upon a huge set of stairs that was rotating and moving! I thought it was the craziest thing in the world. I tried to put my foot on it, but it was moving so fast that I pulled my foot back. I was freaking out just thinking of going on it. People were waiting behind us looking at us expectantly. I looked at Dominic, but he was just as scared as I was. We took the regular stairs.

After we went downstairs, we found a huge wheel that was turning around and around. Dominic went up to it and grabbed two bags as it spun around. I shook my head as I watched people walk around grabbing bags off of the wheel as if it were no big deal.

A woman was standing by the doors that went outside. Dominic gave her a hug and introduced her to all of us as his sister. She held the door open for us as we all walked outside. When I stepped outside I was hit by the most extreme cold I had ever felt. I could feel it like little needles piercing my skin.

Suddenly my breath was taken away. Not from the cold, but because there was snow everywhere. Many of the things I had just seen were strange and unfamiliar, some of them terrifying, but this was the most amazing thing I had ever seen. It was so beautiful.

I had heard the word "snow" before. My mom had told me that I would get to see snow in America, but I had no idea what it looked like. I stood underneath the falling frozen droplets and felt one land on my skin and watched it melt into water as it rested there.

"Amazing," I whispered.

"When it is cold outside the rain freezes and becomes snow," Dominic's sister explained. I did not know it had to be cold for it to snow. It probably sounds silly that I did not know this, but in Africa we just did not learn about things like that.

CHAPTER 7

The False American Dream

DOMINIC'S SISTER HAD SET US up in an apartment on Riverside Drive in Salt Lake. It was a three-bedroom apartment. I shared a room with Fatimah (Sarah's daughter from her pregnancy when she was 12). Dominic slept in a room with his eight-year-old daughter Yatta and his five-year-old son, Dominic Jr. Sarah slept in a room by herself.

We started school a few days after arriving. I was confused through the whole thing. Everything seemed different and fast paced. On the way home I was sitting by myself on the bus. A Hispanic boy came and sat down next to me. He said hello and offered me a little orange piece of candy in a rapper that said Trident on it.

I chewed it for 5 minutes and was amazed that it still tasted good, and it never disintegrated. *This is the most amazing thing ever!* I thought as I chewed the orange flavored delicacy. I was so happy, until I accidentally swallowed it, and it made me so sad. I would have asked him for another but he was already off the bus. I was worried I would never find out where he got it, and never be able to have it again.

A few days later, I was sitting alone in my room thinking about home when suddenly Fatimah came running into our room crying. I asked her what was wrong, but before she could answer, Dominic burst through the door and started hitting and slapping her. I was terrified. I did not know if I should try to help or if I should run. I was still trying to decide, when all of a sudden Dominic turned towards me. There was a crazy look in his eyes, almost animalistic.

I started stepping backward towards the door, but before I could turn and run, he dove forward and slammed into me full force. I was smashed to the ground next to my bed. The wind was knocked out of my lungs. I started to yell for help, but no words came out. He started slapping me in the face over and over again. Each time he hit me, I felt a sharp sting on my cheek.

"You wicked girls!" he screamed as he continued to slap my face and shove his knee into the side of my stomach. When my breath returned, I started crying uncontrollably. I was crying so loudly and trying to get away so furiously that I could not hear what else he was saying. Finally he got off of me and shoved me in the side with his foot. He looked at Fatimah and stepped towards her as a warning. She shrank back submissively on her bed, and he turned and left the room.

Fatimah got up and ran out of the room. I sat up and winced at the pain in my side where his knee had been. I wiped my nose and felt the warm wetness of blood on my finger.

What just happened? I thought. *Is this something that is going to happen all the time?* I was hungry and I had not gone to the bathroom yet, but I was too scared to leave the room. So I slipped into my bed, and quietly cried myself to sleep.

During the following days, Dominic did not hurt me again, but it became clear that things were not going to be very pleasant for me in the Vandi home. Dominic told me that he did me a favor in bringing me to America, and that in return I was to do all of the cleaning in the house.

It was my job to do the dishes. It was my job to pick up everybody's dirty clothes. It was my job to clean the floors, toilets, counters, and to dust everything. I do not even know why they wanted me to dust their ugly things; it did not make them look any better.

I will never forget how gross it was to clean their toilet. All he gave me was a sponge and some soap. He made me get out every stain. I remember dipping my bare hand in the brown water and scrubbing while I tried to stop myself from throwing up.

I learned quickly that Dominic did not care about me. When I would ask for anything or showed any sign of being sad he would tell me how ungrateful I was. He would tell me that he had spent so much money on me, and how I should be so happy for everything that he had given me.

I soon realized I was not part of this family. I was a tag-along. I was not there out of the goodness of Dominic's heart. I was there because he had a family visa, and without his daughter they would have had to redo paperwork. Or maybe he just wanted a slave to make his new life in America even better than he already thought it would be.

Whatever the reason, this was my life. My family was an ocean away. I did not know anybody except for the family I was serving, and I was living in constant fear of being beaten again. I know that I did not have it as bad as many people. I have heard many sad stories, but at the time, I was just a little girl who missed her mom and dad. I missed my life. America was such a wonderful fantasy for everybody else, but for me it was a nightmare.

I felt so alone. I wanted to go and play with Fatimah and her friends, but after we all got back from school. I had to clean the house. By the time I was done it was dinner time. After eating they would go and play again while I cleaned the kitchen. It took me forever because I had to hand scrub and dry each dish. (Dominic said using the dishwasher was too expensive.) By the time I was done they were either gone again or in the middle of a game, and I was left out. I felt like such an outcast.

I changed a lot during those months at the Vandi's house. Probably the biggest change was how quiet I became. When I was a young girl, I talked all the time. I always had something to say. My mom used to tell me that I should be a lawyer, because I could talk and talk, but as I lived with the Vandis, I started to realize they did not care what I said.

Growing up, when I would gab and gab in front of my mom she would just zone me out, but if Dominic and Sarah did not like what I said they would yell at me. When they yelled I became terrified that Dominic was going to hit me again, so I learned to keep quiet and hope they would leave me alone. I became a shadow of myself.

At first I was at least the same girl quietly hiding, but as time went on I stopped being that happy girl. Even when I was alone, when I was not cleaning or being verbally abused by the Vandis, I stopped being happy.

When my parents could afford it, they would buy a phone card and try to call me. When they would call, Dominic would tell them I was gone somewhere, and that I was doing fine.

On my birthday, they told me I could talk to my parents, but they stood next to me while I talked. When I heard my mom's voice, I immediately started to tear up.

"I love you," she said.

"I love you, too," I said.

"Are you having fun? How is school going?" she asked.

I wanted to tell her what was happening. I wanted to ask her to let me come home. I looked up at Dominic; he had a hard mean look on his face. The message was clear. If I said anything about what was going on, I would regret it.

"I am doing really good," I lied as Dominic grabbed the phone away, and that was it. I thought that talking to my mom would make me happy, but the truth was it only made me feel worse--to remember the wonderful family I had left behind.

I was drowning, I felt like the happy part of my soul was leaking out of my body and leaving me in despair. The only thing that brought me joy was talking to my Father in Heaven. I would pour my soul out to him, and I knew He heard me. He was the only one that heard me.

CHAPTER 8

Surviving

DAILY LIFE WITH THE VANDIS was contentious to say the least. They were the complete opposite of a happy family. Dominic was so paranoid and constantly thought he had to defend himself. Most fights would start the same way. Fatimah would quietly say something or just sing a quiet song to herself. It did not matter what she said. It could be "oops, I left my bag in my room," or something simple like that. If Dominic could not hear every word said, he would think she was talking about him.

Inevitably, he would freak out at her and demand that she tell him what she said about him. Usually she was not talking about him, so she would tell him what she had said and he would not believe it. Then he would swear at her and call her names, at which point Sarah would jump in and defend Fatimah. Then Sarah and Dominic would yell and swear at each other.

Sarah would say dirty things about Dominic's mother, and he would scream at the top of his lungs about what a wicked woman she was. Most of the time he would come and find me, he would tell me what happened and try and get me to be on his side since Fatimah was on Sarah's side. Sometimes the yelling would literally last for hours. I would try and get as far away as I could because the contention and loud screaming was just too much for me to handle.

This was just one of the ways fights would start. Another way was even more ridiculous. Because of Dominic's para-noia, he always thought that people were trying to poison him. He was sickly skinny because he would not eat anything that Sarah made. He thought she was trying to kill him.

When he did eat something she made, he would get a stomach ache and then they would fight all night about how she was trying to kill him. The next few days they would completely ignore each other and he would live on Cup-o-Noodles for every meal. He was just such an angry person. I truly think he was mentally ill.

Life continued like this for months. I was beginning to get used to the fact that they did not care about me, but for some reason I was still surprised when nobody came to my junior high graduation.

In truth I do not even know why I wanted them there. I guess I just felt so left out as I watched people wave to their families and give them hugs. I had to accept that I would never have that life. I had to accept that I was alone and I could not depend on them for any happiness.

That summer, I decided I wanted things to be different. I wanted to have some new clothes to wear when I got to high school. I wanted a fresh start. So I started doing hair for some of the girls I knew from the African community. I worked hard to do as much as I could. I really wanted to feel like I fit in when I got to high school.

One day after I got back home from doing someone's hair, Sarah saw me counting the money in my purse.

"You really should put that somewhere safe Victoria," she said. "If you carry it around in your purse, it could get stolen. Do you want me to hold onto it for you to make sure you do not lose it?"

"Okay," I said and handed her the money. I continued to give her the money throughout the summer as I worked towards my goal of buying new clothes for school.

When school was about to start, I was so proud of myself. I was so excited to buy new clothes. I had earned almost $300 and I was ready to spend it.

"I am ready to go shopping for school now," I said as I went into Sarah's bedroom. "You can give me the money back now."

"You did not give me any money Victoria," she said with a blank stare as she sat on her bed.

"Yes I did!" I said as my heart sank. "I gave you almost three hundred dollars"

"You really need to keep better track of your money Victoria," she said with a hint of a smile curling up.

I turned around and slowly walked to my room. I was so frustrated. I was so angry. What was the point? No matter how hard I tried I could not make my situation better. I could not believe I allowed her to trick me. Thinking back on all of those hours doing hair and how sore my hands were, I could not stop myself from crying.

Later that night, Fatimah came into our room with bags full of clothes and school supplies. "Look at all of this great new stuff my mom bought me!" she said excitedly.

I stared at her as she unloaded the bags. New pens, new notepads, a new backpack, new jeans, new blouses, and the list went on and on. I could not take it anymore. I ran out of our room and sat down in the family room just in time to see Dominic Jr. and Yatta unload their bags full of new things. New things bought with my money.

I wanted to cry so badly, but I knew if I did Sarah would yell at me like she always did when I would show too much emotion. She would always remind me of how much they had done for me and how ungrateful I was.

When high school started, I wore the same ratty clothes I had come to America with and any that Fatimah wanted to get rid of after she got her new ones. I was hoping with new clothes I could at least fit in at school. At least then I would feel like I had somewhere that I felt good about myself. But Fatimah was the one that got all of the new clothes.

Later during the school year, Dominic's brother came and visited us from Africa. He brought things for everyone. I was so excited to see him pull out a big package from his duffle bag that had my name on it. My real name: Christiana Karimu.

He was about to hand it to me when Dominic snatched it out of his hands.

"I will need to look through that," he said.

He and Sarah then dug through the box taking out handfuls of African candy and putting it aside. Sarah grabbed a stack of pictures and quickly looked through them before stuffing them in her pocket. She then pulled out five African outfits.

They were the really nice, homemade kind that my mom would make when she could afford material. Four of them looked really cute and the other one was okay, but was made out of cheaper material. Honestly, I was amazed my mom could afford to make any of them. Sarah took the four nice ones and put the one made out of cheap material back in the box and gave it to me.

The dress was all that was left. If that was all that my mom had sent I would have been really happy to have it, but after seeing all of the other fun things in the box, I could not help but feel cheated.

I remember her walking around the house in the dresses my mom made for me. It made me cry seeing the only things my mom had sent *me* being worn by her.

Of course they ate all of the African candy she sent, but what really broke my heart is that they would not let me look at the pictures of my family that were in the package. I do not know what they did with them, but I know that I never got to see them. I asked them a few times where they were and they just ignored me.

One of the friends I had from the African Community was named Howa. Sometimes, when I could, I would spend time at her house. She also came from Sierra Leone after the war, so we had a lot in common. Towards the end of that school year her sister Emma felt bad to see me always wearing ratty looking clothes to school. So she secretly took me to the store and bought me a pair of jeans and a couple of shirts. It was the first time since I had arrived in America that I ever had brand new clothes.

She dropped me off a few blocks away from my house so that they would not see I had been with her. I stuffed the clothes into my backpack and quickly ran to my bedroom. I locked the door behind me and got my little suitcase with the elephant on it out of the closet and tucked the clothes safely inside. I loved that I had these new clothes, but honestly I did not know when I would get the chance to wear them, because if they saw me wearing them, I was sure they would take them away and call Emma and yell at her.

Towards the end of that year, Sarah had a baby, they named her Miatta. Just like everything else in the house the baby became my responsibility. I would bathe her, change her diapers, feed her, and do everything for her.

Adding this to my chores that I was already doing for everybody else made it nearly impossible to do my homework, and having fun was officially out of the question. There was just not enough time.

CHAPTER 9

Hopeless

AFTER THAT YEAR, WE MOVED to a house that the government was paying for us to rent in Taylorsville. While Dominic and I were driving a load of boxes to the new house he revealed that he wanted to bring my sister here instead of me. He said that he had wanted her because she was more mature and more ready to satisfy his sexual needs, including giving him more children. He said that that was the reason I was here was to become his next wife as soon as Sarah was too old to enjoy anymore.

As he spoke, I just stared out the window not knowing what to say. Suddenly we started smelling a really gross burnt smell and Dominic realized he had accidentally left his emergency brake on. He started yelling at me telling me that I should have known better and I should have told him that it was on.

I did not know what to say. I did not know anything about cars, so I just said I was sorry. He just gave me a really angry look and started unloading the car. I was sad that he was getting mad at me for something that was not my fault, but I was glad to have something that distracted us from the conversation we were having.

For some reason once we were settled in at the new house, Sarah decided she did not want anything to do with Miatta. In the past I was only required to watch Miatta during the times that I was not at school, but now they told me that I was not allowed to go to school unless I found somebody else to watch the baby, because neither of them was willing to watch her.

It was my sophomore year and I was now attending Taylorsville High. Because of the baby, I started falling really far behind in school. I started to get desperate. I walked around the neighborhood at seven in the morning knocking on doors asking if anybody was willing to watch the baby for me so I could go to school. Almost everybody gave me a really weird look and said no. They all probably thought it was my baby.

Luckily, I knocked on the door of a woman named Erica; she was so nice about it. She took the baby so I could go to school. She continued to do this from then on. Without her, I probably would have had to drop out of high school.

A few weeks after moving I was invited to go to girls' camp by the local church leaders. I do not know why, but Dominic allowed me to go. It was a nice break to feel like a normal girl. I hate camping, but compared to the Vandi's, it was heaven. The day

I came home, Dominic and Sarah had been fighting all week and apparently were not speaking to each other. The stress of watching their own baby for a week was probably getting to them.

I went down to my room to unpack. Dominic came in and shut the door behind him.

"I bought you some new clothes," he said as he showed me a plastic bag.

He opened the bag and pulled out a mini skirt and a tank top. They looked way too small and skimpy. He handed them to me and smiled at me in a way that made me feel very uneasy. He left my room and I put them away. I did not plan on ever wearing them. They were way too immodest.

Later that week, I was taking care of Miatta like usual. I gave her a bath and fed her and started putting her down for a nap. I was lying in Sarah's bed with the baby, trying to get her to fall asleep, eventually we both drifted off. I woke up and Dominic was standing next to the bed looking down at me with that same creepy smile. He was only wearing his boxer shorts. I ran past him down into the basement.

For some reason I felt like he was about to do something to me, or worse maybe he had already done something. I sat down on my bed and prayed that nothing happened while I was sleeping. I asked God to keep him away from me.

Life continued and I was starting to feel like maybe he really would leave me alone. Damon, a boy I knew from the African community, asked me to be his girlfriend. I was surprised that he wanted to be my boyfriend because he was 18 and I was only 14.

I liked the idea of having a boyfriend so I said yes. We never went on any actual dates. He just took me along with him everywhere while he hung out with his friends. I told him that my parents could not know I had a boyfriend and he could not call me at home. So he gave me a cell phone so he could get a hold of me.

One night I was hiding in the backyard talking to my friend Lynn on the phone. Suddenly, Sarah came into the back yard and caught me on the phone.

"Where did you get that phone?" she yelled. "Did you steal it? Give it to me right now!"

I did not want to give it to her because then she might find out who it belonged to. If she read the texts and found out I had a boyfriend, things could get really bad.

I went inside as she continued to yell at me. I ran downstairs to my room and shut the door. I hid the phone in the ceiling on top of one of the white panels. After I hid the phone I sat down on my bed. I felt so sick to my stomach. What were they going to do to me? A knock came at the door. I opened it up and Dominic was standing there.

"Where is the phone?" he said.

I reached up in the ceiling and brought it to him. He took the phone and went up stairs and talked with Sarah for a little while. I was so scared, wondering what they were planning on doing to me. I thought he was going to beat me up again or maybe throw me out of the house. I did not want to live with them, but I also did not want to be homeless. As awful as their house was, it was all I knew.

Another knock came at my door. Dominic came back in. He had a strange look on his face as he shut and locked the door behind him.

"We are going to sue your boyfriend for rape and he is going to go to jail," he said. "Take off your shirt so I can see if he raped you."

I was too terrified to say no. I did not know what to do. I did not want to find out what he would do to me if I did not do what he said, so I took off my shirt.

"And your bra too," he said.

I hesitated and then took off my bra. He reached over and grabbed both of my breasts in his hands. My body went rigid. What was happening? He just stood there groping my breasts for about two minutes. I did not know what was going on. I did not know what to do. I was scared to stop him, because at this point I did not know what he might do next.

He had a sick look on his face as he stared at my chest. I closed my eyes and tried not to think about what was happening. *Please make it stop* I begged to my Heavenly Father.

He finally stopped and without saying anything he went out of my room and upstairs. I went and sat on my bed and started crying. What did I just do? I felt so guilty. I wondered if it was my fault. He touched me. He took away the one thing I had left. They had already taken my family away, they had forced me to take care of their family like a slave, and now he wanted more. He always wanted more. I hated him. I hated him so much.

I laid there for hours. I was so scared that he would walk through that door again to do more things to me. I was so grateful that Fatimah shared a room with me; if it were not for that I am sure he would have come back. I do not know how, but eventually I was able to fall asleep.

The next day I was upstairs in the kitchen. Sarah was gone. I was doing the dishes when Dominic came in and walked towards me. My body tensed up. I was so scared of what he might be planning.

"I will give you everything you have ever wanted if you will break up with your boyfriend and be with me instead," he said as he stood behind me. I did not say anything. I just stood there and listened, hoping he would go away.

"I will give you everything if you choose me," he said again. I could feel his breath on the back of my neck as he spoke. He was so gross.

I continued to be silent. Neither of us said anything more. I closed my eyes and said a prayer that he would leave. I could tell how angry he was. Finally he left the room. I exhaled gratefully and my fear started to subside. A few seconds later I heard the front door open and close. He was gone.

That day I decided to hang out with my boyfriend after school so that I would not need to go back to the Vandi's right away. After I got out of school he came and picked me up.

We drove to his brother's house. I thought we were going to go hang out with his brother.

When we came through the door his brother saw us, and gathered some things off of the table and left. I was alone with Damon. We walked in and I sat on the couch. He sat next to me, but then got up and walked towards the door. I thought maybe he had left something in his car and was going out to get it, but instead he locked the door.

He came back and sat next to me again. Suddenly he pushed me downward so that I was lying on the couch. Before I could really react, he climbed on the couch and laid on top of me. *What is he doing?* I naively thought. I started to push against him so that I could get up, but he put all of his weight into me and started thrusting himself down into me. I was so scared as I finally realized what he was trying to do.

He reached down and started to take off my pants and I started crying.

"Please stop," I begged "Please do not do this, I want to go home, Please take me home." I tried to get up, but he just kept pushing me down harder. "Stop! No!" I cried. He did not listen.

"You are supposed to love your boyfriend," he said angrily. "If you love me, you will stop complaining. Just be quiet and let it happen."

It did not matter what I said, he would not stop. He would not let me leave. He raped me that night. It hurt so much. I cried the whole time. After he was done, I limped to the bathroom and locked the door. I sat on the toilet and continued to cry. I could not control myself. I just kept crying and crying. I must have been in there for over an hour.

I felt so ashamed. I felt so dirty. What just happened? Why did he do this to me? After I came out of the bathroom he drove me home. We did not say a word to each other the whole drive home. I just sat there staring out the window, wondering why these things always happened to me, wondering if it was my fault.

Even though I was in pain, I knew I could not tell anybody, because Dominic might find out and then he would think it was my fault. He would blame me and hurt me. When I got home, I went downstairs and sat in my room, and stared at the wall. I never felt so alone.

A few weeks later, I earned another honor roll card at school. I usually got one at the end of each term. When I got home I wanted to show it to Dominic and Sarah because I wanted them to be happy for me. I found them sitting on the couch.

"I got on the honor roll," I said expectantly.

Neither of them said anything. They acted like I was not there. I do not even know why I wanted them to be proud of me. I just wanted to feel like somebody was there for me. I went to my room and shut the door.

Later that night I was in my room sitting on my bed looking at all of the honor roll cards I had collected. I smiled as I saw them laid out on my bed. I had something to be proud of. Suddenly I heard someone stomping down the stairs. There was a loud pound on the door.

"Victoria! Give me those honor roll cards," Dominic demanded.

"I earned them," I said. "I should get to keep them."

"You are so ungrateful!" he yelled. "You are nothing! You are a childish whore!"

I curled up in a ball under the covers on my bed and tried to block him out as he continued to yell and call me names that I do not want to repeat. I just wanted to disappear. He continued to pound on my door and yell for almost an hour.

"Stay in your room you dirty prosti-
tute!" he screamed. "I do not want to see
you come out!"

And he was finally gone. As I laid there
in the darkness I could not stop thinking of
my mom and dad. They would have been so
proud of me. The way they treated me was
so good. I laid there whimpering, wishing I
could wake up and be back in Africa with
my parents. Again, I slept on a wet pillow.

CHAPTER 10

My Prison

DURING THE FOLLOWING WEEKS, DOMINIC and Sarah would not allow me to leave my room. When I needed to go to the bathroom, they would not let me go into any of the bathrooms in the house.

"Your parents are not sending us money for the water bill," they would say.

I would go to the neighbor's house to use their bathroom. Sarah and Dominic also would not let me wash my clothes, shower, or eat. I would spend my days sitting in my bedroom. I was so hungry. I hated feeling so dirty. I just wanted to take a shower and wash my clothes, but they would not let me.

The only place I ever was able to eat was at the school. I would eat as much as I could hoping it would last until the next day. Weekends were the worst. I felt like I was going to die. Sometimes I was able to sneak out in the night and get something when everybody was asleep, but most of the time I was too scared of getting caught and beaten.

One weekend I was so hungry. I had lost so much weight. I felt like I was going to die. When I finally felt like I could not take the hunger any more, I snuck out and went to Erica's house. She gave me dinner and I ate like it was my last meal.

"Is everything okay?" she asked. "Are you getting enough to eat at home?"

"No," I said. "They will not let me have any of the food." She was the first person I told. I was so terrified that she might tell somebody else and Dominic would find out, but I had to tell someone.

"You need to talk to the bishop," she said. "He might be able to help you." She wrote down the address of the bishop and told me how to find his house.

"Thank you" I said as I got up to leave. She came and gave me a long hug. At first I was rigid. I did not know how to react to affection anymore. But after a moment, I started to cry and I hugged her back, relishing the feeling that somebody really cared about me.

The next week I was able to sneak over to the bishop's house late one night. I knocked on the door and he invited me in. We sat down and I told him what was going on. I told him the whole story about how they would not let me eat or use any water.

"I cannot help you," he said after I finished my story. "This is a family problem and I cannot get involved. Here is the phone number for child services. I would feel more comfortable if you worked this out with them."

He handed me the paper that he wrote the number on, and got up and started walking toward the door. I left feeling very deflated; I really thought he would help me.

The next day at school I was talking to my friend Linn during our ESL class. I told her the whole story. It was the first time I told her that anything was wrong.

"You should tell Mrs. Farr," she said.

Chalise Farr was the teacher of the class. I was so desperate, I was finally to the point that I would tell anybody. I walked up to the desk and asked her if I could talk to her about something. Class was about to end and so she had me wait until the other students left the room. As I stood there waiting, I had the worst butterflies in my stomach. Linn stayed with me while I told Chalise what was going on.

Except this time, I did not just tell her about the food. I told her about how Dominic was not really my father. I told her about all of the abuse. I told her everything. As I talked, I felt like I was unloading a thousand pounds of bricks off of my back. Every word was another brick. It felt good to tell someone the whole story, but at the same time I was worried.

I was scared because I was not allowed to tell anybody that Dominic was not my real dad. That was one thing that they told me I was never to tell anybody. I was crying as I finished the story. I was so scared to tell somebody. She was so caring and obviously wanted to help.

"What can I do to help?" she asked.

"I do not know," I responded.

She took me downstairs. Her mom worked in the Career Center at the school. Lynn went on to her next class, but Chalise and I went downstairs to talk to her mom.

When we went into her mom's office, I sat down and I told her the same story I had just told Chalise.

She looked at me as I told the story and there was a familiar look in her eyes. It was the same way my mother looked at me when I was hurt or sad. Her name was Kathy. I could just feel that she cared. As strange as it was having just met her, I could feel that she loved me.

They decided the best thing they could do to start with was get me some food to take home and hide in my room for nights and weekends.

That Thursday, they brought me so much food. I filled my backpack with chicken in a can, fruit snacks, crackers, and many other things. I was so happy to have food to take home. I gave Kathy and Chalise a big hug.

I hurried home and ran into my room. I started unloading the food into my closet, when suddenly my bedroom door burst open. Dominic came in and without saying a word to me, gathered up all of the food and walked out.

I just sat there on my knees wondering how he found out about my food. I did not say anything to anybody, the only thing I could imagine is that he saw how excited I looked when I came home and wanted to come and find out why I was so happy.

The next morning I changed into the least dirty clothes I could find and started to go towards the front door to leave to school.

"You cannot go to school today," Sarah said as I reached for the doorknob.

"I have to go to school or I might miss a test," I said as I opened the door to leave. Suddenly, Sarah slammed into me and pushed me against the door and onto the ground.

Dominic followed behind her and started hitting me in the back of the head. I tried to turn over and defend myself but they kept on slamming me back into the ground and hitting me in the back of the head. Sarah kicked me in the side and they finally let go.

I scrambled to the door and tried to get out, but as I opened the door Sarah threw her body against it and slammed my finger in the door. I started to scream in pain, but Dominic wrapped his hand around my mouth to stop me. He started hitting me in the stomach with his other hand while Sarah continued slapping me in the head.

This was not like last time. I could feel that if I did not get out now, I might never get out. I could feel their hatred. *They might kill me!* I thought as I desperately tried to get away.

I kept on wiggling free only to get slammed into a wall or the ground and punched and kicked again. I could not get out! My finger was bleeding like crazy. Sarah grabbed my throat and dug her nails into it. I gasped as I felt each of her nails puncture my skin. I jerked my head away and her nails tore across my neck leaving big cuts. They started bleeding too.

I was hurting everywhere. I felt so dizzy, but I refused to stay down. They may have forced me to serve them, they may have starved me, ignored me, and insulted me, but I would not give up and just let them beat me to death I was going to get out.

I finally ripped my arm free from Dominic but they both grabbed onto my backpack. I was able to get one arm out of it and then the other. They fell backwards and I ran out the front door. I limped across the street and knocked on the door of our neighbor Erica. When she answered I asked if I could use her phone. I could see the worry in her eyes as she said yes and let me in. I called the police on her home phone.

When they answered the phone I told them where I was and what happened. They said they would send someone over. I stayed at Erica's house while I waited for the police to arrive.

Eventually two cop cars showed up in front of the house. I came outside and they asked me to tell them the story. I told them everything that happened that day. After I finished telling them the story they asked us to go inside. One of the officers got out a first aid kit and bandaged up my hand.

The other officer asked Dominic to tell them his side of the story. He told them that I had been stealing money from them and that they were asking for it back, but that I would not give it to them. He said that they tried to get it out of my bag, but I would not let them. Dominic claimed that I had gotten hurt because I wrestled my bag away from them and fell on the ground.

They said that I was pulling on one side of my backpack and trying to slam the door and they were pulling on the other, and that

I shut the door on my own hand trying to shut them in and pull my backpack out.

They said all of my injuries came due to my own carelessness of wrestling the backpack away from them and trying to steal their money. Dominic grabbed my backpack and took out five hundred dollars of cash. The cops did not ask any more questions. They said this is a family problem, not a crime. One of the cops offered to drive me to school. I got in the car and we did not talk at all on the way there.

When we arrived, I got out of the car and went straight to the Career Center and told Kathy everything that had happened. She arranged for me to meet with the school police officer. I told him everything that was happening at home. He wrote it all down, but I could tell he could not help.

After that day, things continued to get worse. They said, "Your parents are not paying us money so we cannot afford food for you" If I left my room, they would push me back in. They would not let me do anything but sit in my room.

Now not only would they not let me use our bathroom, but they would not let me out of the house to ask a neighbor. Because I had not eaten all weekend, I did not need to go during the day, but when nighttime came and they were finally asleep, I could not wait any longer. So, I would sneak out of the house and ask Erica if I could use her bathroom. She always said yes. I do not know what I would have done without her.

CHAPTER 11

A Light at the End of the Tunnel

I CALLED CHILD SERVICES THAT week from the telephone in my church building while I was at a young women's activity. They came the next day and did not talk to me at all. They talked to Dominic and then they went to the school and called me into the counseling center.

"Everything looks perfectly normal at your house Victoria," the woman said. "I spoke at length with your father, and I think everything is going to be alright."

I walked away from the meeting feeling dazed. Why didn't anybody want to help me? I was begging for someone to help. The only people that believed me were Kathy & Chalise, but they could not change my situation alone.

I did not know what else to do, so I called again a few days later and the same thing happened. They came, looked around, talked to Dominic and Sarah, and then told me I was fine. Everything was piling up. I felt less and less safe at home, and nobody was going to help me.

I felt like everything was closing in on me. It was only a matter of time before Dominic and Sarah would attack me again, or worse. Dominic might try to touch me again or rape me. I decided I would rather die than be raped by him, and I knew it was only a matter of time.

The only other option was to kill myself. I was trying to decide how and where to do it, but something inside of me told me to call child services one more time. So I decided to give them one more chance.

This time they sent a girl named Lynny. She came to the school and talked to me. She asked what was going on. I told her the whole story.

Then I told her, "I am done calling you guys. You do not believe me, and you do not care about me." I started to cry. "I do not care what happens to me anymore and neither do you. I am going to make it all end. I am going to kill myself. That is my only way out."

Lynny looked back at me, and I saw something in her eyes that I had not seen in the others. She believed me. Or at least she wanted to believe me.

She arranged for me to go downtown and see a psychologist. When we got there, we met with a middle-aged man. We all sat in a room together.

"What is going on Victoria?" he asked.

I told him everything that I had told Lynny. I told him that I was done dealing with them. The second I got the chance I was going to kill myself, and I meant it. I could not take them not believing me any longer. I had finally given up. Constantly pleading for help and being rejected had pushed me past my limit.

"I do not want her to go anywhere near that house," he told Lynny. "Do what you need to do to get her out of there."

As we left that meeting, a part of me was really glad that somebody believed me, but the larger part of me had already given up. I cannot really explain it, but I felt like I was sleep walking. I felt like I was watching a movie through my own eyes, but I was not part of it.

Lynny drove me straight from meeting with the psychiatrist to Primary Children's Hospital. While we were waiting in the entryway, Lynny asked me for Dominic's phone number. I gave it to her as she dialed it into her phone.

"Is Dominic available?" she said as someone answered the phone. I could hear Sarah's voice on the other line. She sounded like she was getting angry. "I want to speak to Dominic Vandi," Lynny repeated.

For some reason, Sarah was freaking out. I could hear her yelling over the phone. "I will not let you talk to him!" she yelled. "You people stay away from us!" she screamed. Lynny had hardly said a word.

"You tell your husband not to wait up for Victoria. SHE WILL NOT BE COMING BACK! EVER!" Lynny said sternly. Sarah's incoherent screaming was cut off as Lynny's thumb came down on the end call button.

Despite still being in my daze, I could feel a smile forming on the corner of my mouth. After being abused and ignored by Dominic and Sarah for three years, to hear someone push them around for a change was very pleasing.

I spent that first night at the university hospital in a normal bed. While I was lying there in the hospital bed, I was scared about what might happen next. I could not believe that I was done with the Vandis. That night they started me on an anti-depressant while I was at the hospital.

While I was there, one of the nurses came and took me downstairs to get dinner at the cafeteria. On our way down to the cafeteria, I ran into Dominic's sister. She worked at the hospital.

"You are so ungrateful Victoria," she said "After everything they have done for you, you are a despicable child. I am ashamed to know you." She was talking to me in our language, Krio, so the nurse did not understand that she was saying mean things.

"Okay, time to go," the nurse said as she took me by the arm and led me away.

The next day, I was taken to the University Neuropsychiatric Institute (UNI) in Salt Lake City. It is a mental care facility. After I went inside, a young man brought me some clothes to change into. They took my stuff and took out the draw strings in my sweater and the shoelaces out of my shoes. I did not know why they were doing that, but I hoped I would get them back.

I changed my clothes and then they took me to meet with the psychologist. He explained the rules of the facility and what they do. He said each day you do not get in trouble you progress up, and get more privileges; privileges such as being able to go to the downstairs cafeteria, which had better food.

They took me to my room and introduced me to my roommate. We had our own bathroom with a shower, but there were no locks on the bathroom doors. After I checked in, I had to go to a class. In the class they would give us some scenarios and ask what we would do in them. They had similar classes like that a few times a day.

I felt so nervous. I was starting to feel like I was coming out of my trance a little bit, but I still did not feel like this was all real. I was really shy. I did not want to talk to anybody. I just kept the rules and tried not to get noticed by anyone.

CHAPTER 12

Finally Safe

EVENTUALLY, THE DAY ARRIVED THAT I had to go to court. My case worker drove me to the courthouse in Salt Lake City.

"Make sure you do not tell any lies," she said as we drove. "You need to tell the absolute truth. You cannot tell any lies in court." I rolled my eyes. This was the same woman that came to the house twice and said everything looked fine. She still did not believe me.

When we arrived at the courthouse, we went into a room to meet with my lawyer. He had me tell him the whole story so I told him everything that happened while I lived there. He took notes while I told him the story.

"What do you want to happen today, Victoria?" he asked.

"I just do not want to see them ever again," I said as I looked at the ground. That was the end of the conversation. We went into the courtroom.

We sat down on one side of the courtroom. I looked over to the other side and froze up. Dominic and Sarah were sitting there. I looked away from them as my heart started to race. *What if they make me go back home with them?* I though. *They will for sure kill me this time.* I was just starting to feel like I was safe, and now I was terrified again. I started to hyperventilate just thinking about driving home with them.

After the judge came into the room, my lawyer presented my case. He told the judge what I said was happening, and that our request was to be placed into foster care. He also requested to have a restraining order against the Vandis.

He handed the judge a piece of paper. Judge Valdez looked it over. The whole situation was so surreal. I had never been in a courtroom before, and today I was the center of attention. It made me feel very uncomfortable, especially as my lawyer told everybody all of the awful things that the Vandis did to me.

Judge Valdez sat there quietly for a moment and then asked Dominic what his side of the story was.

"In the war, I lost my daughter. Then a man named Roland came and said, 'This is your daughter,' and showed me Victoria. So, I thought this is my daughter. I believed it because that is what I was told," he said.

Judge Valdez had a really funny look on his face. I could tell he was not buying Dominic's story. I liked him already.

"She has caused all of the problems since she got here," Dominic continued. "She is ungrateful for everything we do for her, and she keeps on locking herself in her room. She causes all of her own problems. She is a totally wicked girl."

The judge looked at him skeptically and said, "Well, she says that you are not her dad. I do not want to have any more questions on the matter. I am ordering a DNA test. We will meet again after the test."

My temporary caseworker took me to go get a test done. They put a cotton swab in my cheeks and then sent me back to University Neuropsychiatric Institute.

A couple of days later, we went back to court. When we were all seated there, Judge Valdez said, "We have the results back and she is not your daughter. I am putting her out of your custody and I do not want you to go anywhere near her ever again." At this moment, Dominic stood up and interrupted the judge.

"I did not know what was going on! She has been lying to us! Her dad lied to us!"

The judge told him to settle down. When Dominic would not calm down, Judge Valdez said, "You two need to leave the courtroom. All you need to know is that you are not to have any contact with this young lady ever again."

They were escorted out of the room. My caseworker had a very surprised look on her face. She seemed so convinced that I was lying. After her more or less calling me a liar over and over again, it was nice to see her in the moment she realized she had made a mistake.

"What do you want us to do Victoria?" Judge Valdez asked.

I shyly looked up. I did not know what to say.

"She wants to become a US citizen," my lawyer interjected.

"Sounds like a good idea to me," he said with a fatherly smile. "We will find you a foster home and start your paperwork. It was nice to meet you Victoria. I will see you soon." We left and went back to UNI.

CHAPTER 13

Foster Care

I WAS AT UNIVERSITY NEUROPSYCHIATRIC Institute for several more days. They told me they were transferring me to a new place. A woman named Vedrana came and picked me up. She seemed nice. I was very happy to learn that she was my new caseworker.

She drove me to a place called the "Group Home." There were several girls my age that arrived at the same time I did. We checked in at the front desk. We were told the basic rules and what our days would look like. A woman then took us into a room with lots of clothes and things for us to choose from. I picked out a few outfits.

After that, they took us to the kids' section of the group home. They had a lot of dolls and teddy bears left over from Christmas.

"Everybody grab one or two if you want," the woman instructed.

It was like I went back in time. I was that little girl again who missed out on my one chance for a new toy in Africa. This time I was going to take one. I snatched a brown teddy bear with a red bowtie off the shelf and held it in my arm. The fur was silky and soft. I closed my eyes and smiled with joy. I had new clothes and my own teddy bear.

We each had our own little room. I was amazed. The room was hardly big enough to fit a bed in it, but it was the first time I had my own room.

After putting my new things in my room I walked into the main living area. I was a little nervous. Nobody knew who I was and

I did not know anybody. I slid into my usual pattern of careful quietness, and sat down as far away from the others as possible.

I went through several therapy sessions and group exercises. When I was asked a question, I would answer as quickly as possible and hope they would not ask me more questions. They had a dentist that they used and they told all of us that we were going to go and get our teeth checked. It was so strange having a man I did not know hold my mouth open and look inside. The dentist looked at my teeth and said that I needed some fillings, so he took me back and had me lay down on a dental chair.

They numbed my mouth with a sharp needle. I cringed at the pain. *I hope it goes away soon* I thought. They hooked me up to what they called "laughing gas" and began prodding and sticking their hands in my mouth. Suddenly I started floating away. I was wondering why they were not grabbing me to hold me down. I was panicking a little because I was worried that they would not catch me in time and I would float away and get lost in the air!

The dentist took off my mask.

"All done," he said. "How are you feeling?"

"I am okay," I said, but I was mad at them because I was wondering why they were going to just let me float up into the ceiling. It was frustrating that he did not even say sorry for almost losing me into the air.

After that, we had dinner and they took me to my room. I laid down and thought of all of the wonderful things I had. I cradled my teddy bear in my arms, feeling its silky fur brush against my cheek, and fell asleep on a dry pillow.

The next day, Vedrana came and picked me up. She drove me to the new school I was going to attend. The school was called something like "The Kids' Place." They showed me around the school and told me

I would start school the next day. Vedrana and I got back in her car and started driving back to the group home.

"How are things going in the group home?" she asked.

"It is going good," I said. I did not really know what to say. I was still so shy and quiet.

"We are looking for a good foster home for you, okay?"

"Okay," I said as I stared at the floor of the car. I liked Vedrana, but I still did not want to admit it. I had been betrayed too many times. I could not afford to trust her.

The next morning I got dressed in one of my new outfits, and went to wait for the bus that would take me to "The Kids' Place." I was the only one that was going on that bus, so I just waited by myself. A van drove up. It picked me up and drove me to the school.

The school was a big brown building. It felt really odd being in there. The only school I was used to was Taylorsville High. I went to the front of the building and they checked me in. After I checked in, they took me to a room to wait. Eventually, more students started coming in. We sat in a big circle and people took turns talking about their life.

They would state their names and what foster home they were in and a little about their life story. The teacher had a book and if you participated then he would give you points in his book.

"Tell us about your life Victoria," the teacher instructed when my turn arrived.

"I used to live in Africa, but now I am here," I said so quietly that I doubt anybody heard me. I then quickly sat down, and stared at the ground. The bell rang after sitting in there for a couple of hours.

"Remember, girls, if you talk and interact during lunch you will earn more points," the teacher reminded as we left the classroom.

Lunch was buffet style. So I grabbed my food and found a place I could eat by myself. Some guys were playing foosball in a room off to the side of the lunch room. It looked like they also had a basketball court.

I did not say a word to anybody. I did not know how to start talking to people. I was just so confused about my new life, and I did not really want to get to know anybody new. I figured that they probably would let me down.

After lunch, they taught us some really easy math and other stuff that seemed like it was for someone half my age. We did some simple reading, and then my teacher handed me a card.

"This is for you to take home," he said. I looked at the paper. It had some questions on it about how I did at the group home. "Give it to the group home leader," he instructed. The same van took me back to the group home at the end of the school day,

Apparently If I did well at the group home then I would get more points. I had no idea what these points got me, so I did not try to earn them, I just kept quiet. I am guessing they wanted to teach us how to act normal again. Lots of these girls were like me. They had been abused and learned to be quiet. These people at The Kids' Place wanted to help us break out of the quiet lifestyle that we had put ourselves in.

I did the same thing the next day. A few days later, Vedrana came and she and I sat down. "We found two good options for a home for you. One of them is in Tooele. That one might be good because Jessica, one of the girls that is here with you, is going to be there."

"That's good," I said, but I was thinking that I did not want to be with that girl. She was part of one of the cliques in the group home and she was always fighting with other girls and swearing at them.

"The other one is in Murray. If you choose the Tooele one, then the girl that is here with you will be your roommate," she said.

"If I go to Tooele, will I be able to go to Taylorsville High School?" I asked.

I wanted to stay where Kathy was. I knew that she would watch out for me, and she was the only person I felt like I could trust. She was the only person that I felt like loved me.

"If you go to Tooele you will not be able to go to Taylorsville. It is too far. If you go to Murray, there is a chance you could go to Taylorsville," she said. "Do not decide yet. Each family is going to come and visit you first."

Later that day, I was called to the front desk. I walked there and they took me into a room to meet with one of the families. I went in and met a woman in her mid-40's.

"We will take good care of you. We have movie nights as a family once a week. Sometimes we go out to eat, all of us together. Doesn't that sound like fun?" she said with an expectant smile on her face.

"You will have some chores to do, but not very many. Jessica will be your roommate, and you will go to Tooele High School."

That is where she lost me. I did not want to live with Jessica, let alone be her roommate. Besides, I wanted to go to Taylorsville High School. I waited through the rest of the meeting and eventually she was done telling me about the home.

"It was very nice to meet you Victoria," she said and shook my hand "We hope we get to see you very soon."

I smiled at them and they left with Vedrana. When I walked out after them the family was talking to the people at the front desk. I went back to the play area and sat down on one of the couches.

"Wow! We are going to be in the same home!" Jessica said as she approached me. "We are going to have so much fun and share clothes and do lots of fun things." I just smiled at her and did not say anything. "We are going to be like sisters, aren't we?" she said expectantly.

"Yeah," I said with little enthusiasm. After ignoring me this entire time, all of a sudden she thought we were best friends.

I went back to my room and waited for bedtime. The next day I was able to call Vedrana. I told her that I could not go to Tooele because I needed to stay at Taylorsville High School. I needed to stay with Chalise and Kathy.

The next day I was called in again. There was a woman named Susan there.

She brought her biological children Mandy and William with her.

"How are you doing?" Susan asked.

"I am good," I said as I half smiled and looked at the ground.

"I currently do not have any foster girls at my house. Sometimes we have two or three, but right now we do not have any. You will have your own room and it is pretty big," she said.

"Can I go to Taylorsville High School if I live with you?" I asked, deciding to be a little more straightforward this time.

"I think we could work something out," she said. "We do a lot of fun things. We go to the movies, we go out to eat, you can take piano lessons, or play any sport you want."

She continued talking, but I did not really care about anything else. I was just happy to know that I had a chance to stay at Taylorsville High with Kathy and Chalise.

Later that day I sat down on my bed and started thinking about if I should go to Susan's house. I was kind of amazed that they were leaving it up to me. I could not remember a time in my life that I was allowed to make a major decision.

I liked that Susan said I could go to Taylorsville High if I moved in with them, but I did not really feel like I would fit in at their house.

I called Vedrana and told her I did not really like either of the choices.

"I am sorry Victoria, but they are the only two options right now," she said. "If Taylorsville is what is important to you, then right now, Susan is your only option."

"Ok, I want to go with Susan then," I said.

"Great. It will probably take a couple of days to get it all ready, but then you will be able to move in."

That Friday night at about 11:00 pm, Susan came to get me. It was late because she just got off of her shift at work. We went to Walmart and she helped me pick out some bedding. I picked a fluffy blue blanket with the princess from the Disney show *Princess and the Frog* on it.

We then drove to Susan's house. She showed me the kitchen and the main areas of the house, and then took me to my room. It was a little room in the basement with a mattress on the ground.

"Good night hun," she said with a sleepy smile as she put my bag down next to the bed. And just like that I was in another new place. I could not help feeling a little uncomfortable. It seemed like I was in a new place every day. I laid down and closed my eyes hoping that someday I could feel at home here.

CHAPTER 14

Holly

LIFE AT SUSAN'S WAS DIFFERENT than what I was used to - to say the least. We ate a big dinner every night. We went out to eat and could order whatever we wanted. And we got new clothes and other new things regularly. Despite the changes, I still was not happy. I was glad I was safe, but being happy was a whole different story.

I had only been there for a week, when Susan told me my therapist would be coming to see me. *Therapist?* I thought. *I have my own therapist?* I had therapy sessions while in University Neuropsychiatric Institute, but I did not really feel like they were *my* therapists. They just worked there.

That evening I sat by the window waiting for her to get there. A silver car pulled up and a short girl with blond hair stepped out. She did not look like a therapist. She seemed too young. She came and rang the doorbell. I slowly opened the door.

"Hello Victoria," she said with a big smile. "I am Holly. Are you ready to go?"

I was so shy. I did not say a word. I just nodded and we walked over to her car. We went a couple of blocks and she parked in front of the 7-11 convenience store.

"Do you want a hot chocolate?" she asked smiling again. She had blue eyes, and was very pretty.

"Sure," I quietly said. She seemed so nice, but I still had to be careful. After we got our drinks, we started to drive again.

"What do you like doing?" she asked as she looked forward at the road.

"I like dancing," I said as I sipped my drink carefully, trying not burn my tongue.

"Wow that is fun. What is your favorite subject in school?"

"Math and English," I whispered quietly. I really did not dare to say anything more than answer her direct questions. Dominic was such an angry person; he made me so scared to say anything wrong.

She continued to ask me all sorts of questions. Several times I did not even have the guts to say a response. I would just give a half smile and nod, or shake my head.

We never went anywhere; we just drove all around while we talked. When the hour was up she dropped me off at home and that was it. I went down to my room with a careful smile on my face. *Can I trust her?*

For the next couple of weeks I continued to go to The Kids' Place. One day, I was walking in the hallway when I happened to pass the school office. I saw Kathy in there.

I was so excited. I could not believe she was there. I quickly approached her and gave her a big hug. Feeling the material of her shirt pressed against my cheek reminded me of when I used to bury my face in my mother's dress. Not just the feeling of the material, but the feeling of safety.

"I came to see if you can be transferred to Taylorsville High School. I have been so worried about you," she said. "After you left, they would not tell me anything. They said that I was not family so they could not give out that information. I have been trying so hard to find you. When I found out that the principal from our school was coming to see you today, I came with him because I wanted to see you so much."

I was so happy to have her there. She and Chalise were truly the only people I trusted in the world.

The bell rang. I gave her another hug, and then I walked away with a big smile on my face. She was still here. For once, someone was sticking with me. Someone was fighting for me.

I was at The Kids' Place for another couple of weeks while they were working on transferring me. I met a girl named Katie while I was there. She seemed really nice, and eventually we started eating lunch together and being friends.

During lunch, she would hardly eat anything. It did not seem like enough to get through the day. After she ate she would immediately go to the bathroom and throw all of her food up. One day we were eating lunch and she looked at me with a careful expression.

"Can I tell you a secret?"

"Of course," I said.

"I am bulimic," she said. "Whenever I eat anything, I go to the bathroom and throw it up afterwards."

I was so confused. Living in Africa I could not imagine someone having food to eat and then throwing it up. I spent so much time wishing I had more food. Why would I go and throw it up on purpose?

"Why would you do that?" I asked.

"I do it because I am so fat and I want boys to like me."

"You are not fat at all!" I said.

"No, I am. You are just being nice."

She would always point to different parts of her body and say, "Look how fat I am." I felt so bad that I could not convince her that she looked fine. Eventually, I was released from The Kids' Place and went back to Taylorsville High. I never saw her again.

CHAPTER 15

Foster Care

EVENTUALLY, MORE FOSTER GIRLS MOVED into the house. Susan knew I wanted to keep my own room so she decided to put me in a room right next to the one I had been staying in. Before I moved my things in, I asked her to paint it lime green. I wanted something totally different for my new life. She painted it and I moved in.

Most of the girls in foster care would fight all the time. It seemed like all they wanted to do was get into trouble. I did not really get along with most of them. I remember one of the other black girls that lived there with us used to tell me I was "the whitest black girl" she ever met because I would not do drugs with them.

Whenever I was tempted to try and fit in, I would think of Kathy and how disappointed she would be if I did something wrong. Whenever I thought of Kathy, it helped me be strong and not care what they thought of me or said about me.

There was one girl however that I did become great friends with. Her name was Tyanna We got along really well. She was 15 years old and she and I just clicked. We would stay up late, joking about silly things, and laughing until we cried. I was so happy to have a friend. Tyanna and I definitely did not have the same standards, but she respected my beliefs and I loved her for that.

Suddenly she started throwing up all the time. She seemed to always feel sick.

"I think you are pregnant," I said.

"No, I am not," she said.

Later that month she went to the doctor because she was so sick. She wanted to find out what was wrong. They did some tests and told her that she was pregnant. I went up to her room to talk to her about it.

After she let me in, we sat on her bed like we always did when we talked.

"I have been talking to Susan and my case worker, and I think that I am going to get an abortion," she said

"Why do you want to do that?" I asked.

"I do not know what else to do. If anybody finds out about my boyfriend, he will get in trouble because he is over 18. My caseworker also thinks it is a good idea, because having the baby will ruin my life--especially if I decide I want to keep it."

"The little life growing inside of you is not a problem to be dealt with. It is a little baby. You cannot kill a baby because it is going to make your life difficult. Each baby deserves a chance to live," I said with alarm.

"I do not know, everybody else thinks it is such a good idea to abort the baby. They have all said that they support me in doing it."

"It does not matter what they think. Abortion is wrong. You were given this baby for a reason. This baby is supposed to be born on this earth and he or she is going to affect your life or somebody else's in a major way. Everything happens for a reason and this baby is a blessing not a curse. You cannot kill your own child!" I said with conviction.

We talked a little more about it, but she did not say whether she was going to have an abortion or not. That night I prayed that she would not abort the baby. The next day they called me in for a meeting. Every now and then we would have a meeting with our tracker, foster mom, case worker, and therapist, so I did not really think anything of the meeting.

This time though it was only my tracker Liz, my foster mom Susan, and Tyanna's tracker Lori. When I saw Lori there, I knew something was up.

"You need to mind your own business," Lori said bluntly as I took a seat at the kitchen table.

"We know you mean well Hun, but you need to let Tyanna make her own decisions," Susan added.

I just sat there and listened. This was one thing I was not going to be pushed around on. Murder is wrong.

"Tyanna's pregnancy is absolutely none of your business," Lori continued. "I do not want you talking with her anymore about it. Tyanna has decided to get the abortion, and I want you to stay out of this. Is that understood?"

I sat there and did not say a word. I would not promise to keep out of this. I would not be quiet while my best friend murdered her baby. After they told me I could go, I shot Susan a dirty look and went downstairs to my room.

As I sat in my room, I continued to get angry. I could not believe that Tyanna tattled on me. *Why would she even bother telling them that I had told her not to get the abortion if she was just going to do it anyway? Why get me in trouble while at the same time completely ignoring my advice?* After she got home that night, I went up to her room to tell her what I thought.

I knocked on her door

"I will never butt into your business or your life again," I said loudly, and then went back downstairs and locked myself in my room.

She came and knocked on my door, but I would not answer. She knocked again.

"Please Victoria, please talk to me. It is not what you think."

I still would not answer the door. It was quiet for about 20 minutes, and all of a sudden I heard a knock at the door. I looked over as a piece of paper was slid under my door.

I quietly walked over and picked it up. I had to be quiet because I did not want her to know that I was reading it.

Dear Victoria,

I love you, I think of you as my sister and my best friend. I am sorry if I did something that made you mad. Today I told my tracker that I wanted to have the baby. I told her that I talked to you and that I do not think that an abortion is okay. I did not know that they would get mad at you. Please do not be mad at me.

I put the letter down and felt so bad for being mad at her. I was so happy to hear that she was going to keep the baby. I opened my door and ran upstairs to her room and gave her a big hug.

"I'm sorry," I said. "Lori told me that you were going to get the abortion and that I should butt out of your life."

"Of course not! I would never say anything like that," she said. "I am sorry they got mad at you. I can't believe they lied to you."

From that day forward we grew even closer. I was so happy that she respected my opinion enough to change her life so much because of it. She truly was a good friend.

Another important thing I learned that day was that I could not trust the adults in the foster care system. They would lie right to your face to get their way, and most importantly they had no respect for me as a person. In a way, they were just like Dominic. They treated me like I was of a lesser intelligence than them.

One thing that was different, however, was that I was finally safe. With that safety came peace. I could finally enjoy being a teenager. I was able to enjoy school and I started living life like a regular kid.

I had to take two UTA busses plus one train to get to school every day. Sometimes Susan would take me on her way to work.

When she did this, I would be there about an hour early so I would sit in front of the Career Center and the principal would let me into Kathy's office. Usually I would sleep on the ground in front of her desk.

I liked waking up and seeing her there. I still called her Kathy, but in truth, I felt like she was my mother. Not that she was replacing my mom in Africa, but she was just adding to my life. I felt like I had known her my whole life. She was family.

High school became my life. I finally felt like I belonged somewhere. I was in two school plays, I was in choir, I was on the tennis team, and I always had something going on. I wanted to try a little bit of everything. Chalise was the coach of the track team, so I decided it might be something fun to try hurdles. Susan bought me running shoes and running pants and everything I needed.

I arrived at the practice and Chalise told us to warm up. Some of the kids started running in place and stretching so I tried to copy them. I felt so uncoordinated trying to do the things they were doing.

"We are going to run around the track a few times to get started," Chalise said.

The girls started running and I fell into the pack. When I used to see girls running on the track, it did not look like they were moving very fast. But now that I was there doing it with them, I could barely keep up.

"Lets pick up the pace girls," Chalise said.

I looked over at her wondering what she was thinking. The girls sped up and I was left in the dust. I tried to keep up, but my lungs started burning and I felt like my throat was being crushed.

I stopped running and put my hands on my knees as I dropped my head down. I was breathing so heavily. Chalise told me to take deep breaths and to make sure I did not lay down. I just stood there trying to catch my breath. When I finally was able to calm down, I went and sat down on the bleachers and watched the girls for a little while. Then I left. I never went back to track. I had done enough running in my life.

That is so gross I thought. *I was just a little girl when I was at the Vandi's and he is a full grown man.* He then grabbed me and started rubbing against me.

"Let me go!" I shouted. But he just twisted my skin on my wrist and held me tighter. He pulled me over to the couch and forced me to sit on his lap. He started grinding against me and moaning. I was finally able to wiggle away from him.

"Take me home!" I demanded as I walked toward the front door.

"Come in and lay down for a little while," he said as he opened the door to the bedroom.

"I do not want to," I said sternly. I was not that same little girl that had been taken advantage of so many times. I now knew what it was like to be free from men like this, and I was not going to let him hurt me.

"If you were more mature you would know that when a man takes you to an empty apartment, he expects you do as he says. You would know what you are supposed to do." he said angrily.

"I do not want to do anything with you. I want to get married in the temple to a returned missionary," I said resolutely.

"Fine!" he yelled, as he walked to the front door. He unlocked it and walked out. I said a silent prayer thanking Heavenly Father that Matthew did not try to force me into that bed. I quickly took my chance and followed him out of the apartment.

We got in the car and started driving back the way we came. We never went to see his wife or kids. When we were a few blocks away from my house, he pulled over and tried to kiss me. I tried to pull away, but he planted an awkward one on the side of my mouth as I leaned away. I was so revolted that my lips had touched his. I quickly wiped them with my sleeve.

"Do not tell anybody what happened," he said. "I am proud of you for having high standards."

It was obvious he was trying to get on my good side so that I would not rat him out. I got home and went downstairs and slammed my bedroom door. I was so frustrated; I thought I was done with things like this. I was angry. I felt betrayed, but I did not cry. I had cried too much in my life. I would not shed anymore tears over little people like him.

A couple of weeks later, I heard my friends talking about how one of them was molested. I was confused because I thought that molestation and rape were the same thing. Later that night, I asked Tyanna what it means to be sexually molested.

"It is when somebody touches you or rubs their body on yours when you do not want them to," she said. "Why?"

I told her exactly what happened and who the guy was that did it to me.

"You were definitely molested. You need to tell your therapist," she said.

So I talked to Holly about it at our next therapy session. After I told her what happened, she set up a time to talk to an investigator. Two or three days later she drove me to this place. I sat in a room and talked to a man in a suit.

"Tell me everything that happened," he said as he turned on a voice recorder. I felt very weird and nervous talking about this with a guy I did not know--and especially recording it--but I told him the whole story.

"We will look into it," he said as he turned off the voice recorder and let me out of the room. Before we left the building they let me pick out a stuffed animal.

While we were driving home, Holly asked me if I wanted her to call my bishop, because the guy was in my church ward.

"Yes please," I said. I was happy she was with me during that interview. I really was starting to trust her. She was more than a therapist. She was a true friend.

Later that week my bishop called me and asked to meet with me. When I went into his office, he started crying.

"I am so sorry this happened to you Christiana," he said as he sat at his desk.

I was so amazed. I had never seen anybody cry so hard for me. He could barely get the words out.

"We are going to tell Matthew to find a new ward, okay?"

"Thank you," I said as I started to cry too. I was not crying because of Matthew. I was crying because my bishop believed me.

He really believed me without even asking me any questions. It felt so good to have somebody care for me enough to cry for me. He gave me a big hug.

"Make sure you come and see me whenever you want, okay?" he said as he let go of the hug.

I nodded to him and wiped the last of my tears from my face as I left his office.

The next Sunday I did not go to church because I did not want to run into Matthew. After church time was over I heard a car pull into the driveway. It was Matthew's car! I ran downstairs and told Susan what was happening. We heard banging at the door.

I cowered back as fear started to take over my body. *What is he going to do to me?* I wondered. I wanted to hide. I felt like a little girl again. I wanted to climb under the bed and hide from him, like I hid from the rebels during the war. Susan stomped to the front door and swung it open.

"Excuse me! Why are you pounding on my door?" she asked sternly. I sat at the bottom of the stairs listening.

"I want to talk to Victoria right now!"

"Who are you?"

"I am her uncle," he lied.

"I am pretty sure Victoria does not have any family here. I want you to leave my house right now. And I do not want to ever see you here again or hear that you are bothering her." With that she slammed the door.

I heard a car start, and then he was gone. I relaxed and leaned against the wall. It took a few minutes for my breathing to settle back to a normal rhythm. I was so proud of Susan. Suddenly, it seemed like I had people looking out for me. I was so glad she was there to protect me. I do not know what would have happened if she was not there.

With Kathy and Chalise at school, Susan at home, and Holly visiting regularly, I suddenly had people protecting me. I still had nightmares of the Vandis and the war, but now when I woke up, I found that I was starting to believe things were going to continue getting better.

Sometimes I would run into Dominic's daughter Fatimah at school. She told me that Matthew was telling everybody in the African community that I tried to get in bed with him, but that he stayed true to his wife and told me no. I did not care what he said or they thought. I was just glad he was out of my life forever.

I decided it was time to stop living in the past. That week I asked my caseworker if I could legally change my name back to Christiana, my real name. She said yes, and I left the name Victoria in the past with all of the pain.

CHAPTER 17

Off to College

DURING MY SENIOR YEAR, KATHY helped me fill out a scholarship form for Horatio Alger. She thought my life story might help me win the award.

One day when I was watching T.V., the phone rang. I answered it and they told me that I had been awarded a $20,000 scholarship from Horatio Alger. I was shocked. I could not believe that I had done it.

They told me I would be getting a plane ticket and that I would be traveling to Washington D.C. to receive the check and a plaque during a ceremony. I hung up the phone and called Kathy immediately. She was so proud of me.

When I told Kathy about the trip to Washington, she noticed that it was during the same time as my trip to Disneyland with my school choir. I was pretty bummed that I would be missing my trip, so Kathy offered to take me to Disneyland after school got out.

Sadly, when Horatio Alger found out that I was not yet a US citizen, they had to withdraw the award. They said that the award was only available to US citizens. I was crushed. I was so excited, and so proud to be one of only two students to receive the award in Utah, and now it had been taken from me. Although I did not get to keep the Horatio Alger scholarship. I still felt proud.

Luckily I was used to disappointment and I rebounded quickly. I applied for other scholarships. With Kathy's help, I was able to obtain three smaller scholarships that added up to almost $9,000.

Several weeks later, the Salt Lake Tribune decided to do an article on a student from our school who had overcome a lot. My principal and Kathy told them about me and they decided to do the article on me.

So there I was with a full page story in the May 22, 2010 Salt Lake Tribune. I felt like I was famous. They wrote about some of my trials, but they did not even know the worst parts. Those have been buried inside of me up until now.

Kathy kept her promise and she took me to Disneyland with her family after school was done.

It was amazing. We went on so many rides. I really felt like I was part of a family for the first time since I left home. I continued calling her Kathy, but she knew I thought of her as my mother. Who else would go through so much trouble to protect me and make me happy than my mother?

After we got back from our trip, my caseworker and some other people from the foster care system gave Kathy a really hard time for taking me to Disneyland. They told her she was "overstepping her bounds." She did not care what they said. All she cared about was me, and that trip had made me very happy. I thought it was pretty ridiculous to say that the person that saved me when nobody else would was "overstepping her bounds."

After applying to several different schools, I was accepted to Snow College. Again I was disappointed to find out that because of the confusion with my immigration status I was not able to addend school there. I was crushed, but I again rebounded quickly and began attending Salt Lake Community College or SLCC.

I still lived with Susan while I attended college. I wanted to become a lawyer someday, but to start I was just taking generals. I took the bus to SLCC, just like I did when I would go to Taylorsville High. Some of my classes were night classes, so I had to take the bus late at night.

On more than one occasion a man would pull up and ask me if I wanted to make some money. I could not believe how shameless these men were. Naturally I said no, but sometimes I worried that they were not going to take no for an answer. I strongly believe that on some of those occasions Gods protection is the only reason I was not kidnapped or rapped.

CHAPTER 18

Romance is in the Air

WHILE ATTENDING SALT LAKE COMMUNITY College, I met a boy at school named Mike. He was really nice and always said, "hi" to me when I passed him in the hallway. One day, he saw me waiting at the bus and asked if I wanted a ride home. For the first time ever, I accepted the ride. He was different. He was a good person. We talked about our church and school. Eventually, he mentioned that he had a friend, Brian that I should meet. A week or so later he set up a time for us to go on a double date.

The first time I met Brian, I will never forget his smile. He was so happy and energetic. He was very over the top with his compliments and corny pickup lines. But unlike the other boys I had dated, behind the jokes and cocky things he said, there was a humble man just having fun. I knew from that first night that I wanted to be with him.

I called him several times over the next few days. Usually his mom would answer and tell me he was off somewhere and that he would call me back. He never called back.

Meanwhile, I was getting called every night by a boy I knew named Mohammed. He was constantly pressuring me to date him. I told him I needed to see where things went with Brian first. Mohammed was one of the most popular boys in the African community, and was not used to rejection. He continued to call every day.

When I did get a hold of Brian, he always needed to go and very rarely seemed like he had time for me. Because of that first date, and because I knew he was different, I continued to call. Finally we set up a date. I was really excited. I looked forward to it all week.

The day before our date, he called and apologized over and over again. He told me that he had been called into work and that we would have to reschedule.

He seemed so distraught and apologetic. For a girl that had been stood up by other boys so many times with no real explanation, I actually was even more attracted to him based on the fact that he felt sad that he had to reschedule, and that he told me beforehand rather than just not showing up like the others had. We set up a new date for the next Friday.

I endured several more phone calls from Mohammed; he continually tried to point out how he adores me, and how "this guy Brian does not even seem to care."

He told me all of the right things, but I had heard them before. I needed something new. I needed a man that did not *say* all the right things, but *did* the right things. A man that cared about me, not just himself or his ego.

I waited anxiously for Brian to arrive on the night of our first single date. When the doorbell rang, I was too nervous to answer so I sent one of the other girls to get it. She came and told me he was here. I went up and found him standing in the entryway holding a bouquet of blue-colored daisies. I did not know how to react. Nobody had ever given me flowers before. I told him thank you and we were on our way.

He apologized right off the bat and said he did not have anything special planned. We went to a movie, and afterward, he

Christiana F Crawley

asked where I would like to go to dinner. I was starving, but I told him I was not hungry because I did not want him to see me eat and think I was gross or ate too much.

We drove around awhile looking for a good place to park and talk. It was dark and I had been in this situation before. *Park and talk?* I thought. *Could he be just like them after all?*

We ended up parking by a school baseball field in Salt Lake City. It was pitch dark in the parking lot. I braced myself, hoping he would not try and take advantage of me like every other guy would and had.

"We should get to know each other better," he said as he turned off the car. *Here we go,* I thought. Suddenly, to my surprise, he started asking me question after question. He would then share a few things about himself, but mostly just kept asking about me.

I could not believe that he was not trying to kiss me or touch me. We were there for a couple of hours and he did not even try to hold my hand. As we drove home, he again apologized for not doing anything "fun." I told him it was really fun.

He said he would make it up to me on our next date, and plan something special. Little did he know that was the only "real" date I had ever been on. My old boyfriends would just take me somewhere quiet and try to take advantage of me, or they would take me to their friends' house and totally ignore me until we were alone.

He dropped me off and gave me a side hug goodnight. I stepped inside and was walking on air. I could not believe that a good guy might really exist. I went straight to my room (after eating) and stared at my flowers for hours. He was real, a good man, a man that respected me and was not just looking for action.

I called Mohammed the next day, and told him that "things are different with

Brian; I am going to have a relationship that might actually go somewhere."

It may have been a bit harsh, but Mohammed was no different than the other guys I had dated. I am sure nothing was hurt but his pride. He probably was on the phone with his next girl within minutes, and that was fine with me. I found what I was looking for.

CHAPTER 19

A Dream Come True

THE NEXT FEW WEEKS WERE all about Brian. He was all I could think about. Whenever Brian came to the door, my heart started racing. We had already been on three dates and he still had not kissed me. I was wondering why and he must have known it, because as we were driving to Mike's apartment to watch a movie, he told me why.

"Just so you know, I really want to kiss you. The only reason I am not is because I do not think it is fair to kiss someone until you are ready to commit to a serious relationship. I only want to kiss you if I mean it, not just because you are beautiful. Which you are and that makes keeping my rule even harder," he said with a wink.

He looked at me and smiled. We held hands during the movie that night. After the movie, Mike went in his room and Brian and I sat on the couch and talked for almost two hours. I was so happy that he was so interested in me. I had never met a guy that really wanted to talk about me.

Two days later, on our fourth date, we were standing on my doorstep. He gave me a tight hug and whispered in my ear, "Can I kiss you?"

I did not even answer. I just leaned my head back and let him kiss me. It was the most amazing moment of my life. I never felt so loved and so protected. After he finished kissing me, he gave me a long hug. As he held me tightly in his arms, I knew that

I never wanted to leave his side again. I said goodnight and went inside.

I went downstairs to my green room and laid on the bed. How had my life gone from something so dark to an opportunity so bright? If Brian and I got married, I would go from war, to slavery, to foster care, and into the loving arms of a husband, and a home and family of my own.

After everything that had happened to me, I wondered if it was too good to be true. As silly as it sounds, I frequently feared I would wake up at the Vandi's and all of this would be a dream.

The following weeks were perfect. Brian would come over almost every night, and we would go out to a movie, or for a long drive, or to the park. He would bring me flowers sometimes or little cute gifts. I remember one night after we got back from one of our dates, he seemed to be thinking really deeply about something.

"What are you thinking?" I asked.

"I was just wondering if I should tell you I love you."

I froze up. I knew I loved Brian, but I had not really spent a lot of time thinking about that. I had never believed I would fall in love. I looked into his blue eyes as he looked back at me. I had never trusted anyone the way I trusted him. Did he know that he was holding my fragile heart in his hands?

"I do love you, Christiana," he said with a loving smile.

"I love you too, Brian," I said as tears started to roll down my cheeks. I wiped my tears and buried my face in his shoulder and hugged him tightly.

"Why are you crying?" he asked.

"I just never thought I would love somebody. I never believed I could trust somebody the way I trust you." He pulled me in tighter and gave me a long hug.

"I promise I will never hurt you," he whispered in my ear. And then perhaps the most amazing thing of all happened. I believed him.

I continued to cry. My dreams really were coming true. God had answered my faithless prayers. I did not believe he existed, but I continued to ask for him, and Heavenly Father had given him to me.

When Brian and I started discussing marriage, the opposition that we faced from the foster care system was so extreme. They all were telling me that I was too young to get married. They told me I was throwing my life away.

I was amazed that they were willing to provide me with a bunch of birth control options and send me to college, but somehow getting married was the wrong thing to do. My foster family was so mean to Brian and constantly talked bad about him behind his back.

Eventually I had to tell them that if they kept pushing him away and talking bad about him, I would never come and see them again after we were married. I told them that he was going to be a part of my life from now on, period. If they wanted to be in my life they needed to accept him. After that, they were not necessarily nice to him, but they did stop talking bad about him.

The only person that was in favor of the wedding was my American mother, Kathy. As always, she could see what was best for me. She did not care about what other people said. She could see that I was happy. She saw that Brian cared about me, and that for the first time in my life someone besides her was putting me first.

I will never forget how she said, "I usually am not in favor of getting married this young, but in this case it is absolutely perfect."

I already knew he was going to propose. It was just a matter of when and how. The day before Mother's Day, Brian took me on a little hike to what he called his "Favorite Thinking Spot". He had a bouquet of red roses with him that he said were for his mother.

"Why not just leave them in the car?" I asked.

"I do not want them to get squished by laying on their side," he responded.

I took the flowers from him and counted them.

"There are only 11," I pointed out. He grabbed them from me and counted them.

"What a rip off," he said.

When we arrived at his spot, I was struck by how perfect it was. It was like something straight out of a Thomas Kinkade painting. There was a little bench hidden in a cluster of trees overlooking a small stream. It was perfect.

We sat down and he kissed me tenderly and pulled me in for a hug. I rested my head on his chest, and closed my eyes as I listened to his heart beat.

"Today I lied to you for the first time," he said. "I told you the flowers were for my mom, but they are for you."

He handed me the flowers along with a note. I read it out loud:

Christiana,
   I will love you until the last of these roses wilts.

I thought it was sweet, but wondered if he realized that the roses would soon wilt, and that his note did not make much sense. Suddenly, he pulled out a beautiful rose that was covered in a glossy finish and the stem was dipped in pure gold.

"Here is the 12th rose," he said with a smile. "This is a real rose coated in glass and pure gold. It will never wilt," he said. I pulled him in for a tight hug.

"I want to promise you something Christiana," he said. "I want to promise you that I will love you forever. That I will always put you first, and that I will spend every day trying to make you happy. But in order for me to do this, you need to do something for me."

He leaned back from our hug and got down on his knee. When I realized what he was doing, butterflies filled my stomach.

"You need to marry me," he said as he pulled a ring from his pocket. "So Christiana Karimu, will you marry me?"

I just sat there crying. I could not even speak. Somehow, even though I knew this was coming, I was not prepared. He stood, helped me up, kissed me, and gave me a big hug.

"Yes," I whispered as he held me in his arms.

CHAPTER 20

Getting Ready for the Wedding

THE DAY BEFORE OUR WEDDING, I received a letter from the foster care agency that, in not so many words, said if I got married; I probably would not obtain citizenship for a minimum of ten years and maybe never. It also said I would likely be deported and I would have to live in Africa for at least three years before Brian would ever be able to bring me back.

This was intermingled with a lot of heavy reading and language that was obviously meant to intimidate me. As I read the letter, I became more and more terrified. I thought that there was a good chance they were going to deport me right after I got married. I put the letter on the counter and waited for Brian to come and pick me up.

When he arrived, I showed him the letter. He read over it carefully and looked up at me.

"This is garbage," he said. "They are just trying to scare you out of marrying me. None of this is true. Don't even worry about it."

"How do you know?" I asked.

"Just look at how silly it is," he said. "They hardly even deport criminals, but these people are trying to get you to believe that they will deport someone who was brought here as a child and who was in Utah's foster care system for three years, just because she has the audacity to get married?"

"These people are a total joke and more of a disappointment than even I thought they were, and that's saying something. Do not spend another second worrying about them." He took the letter from my hands and gave me a long hug

"God wants us to be together Christiana, and I know that this letter is not true. But if they did send you back to Africa, I would be going with you and we would be together. Isn't that all that matters?"

Him offering to go to Africa with me if he needed to was all I needed to hear. We put the letter away and he helped me pack up my things to get ready for the wedding.

I often wonder why the foster care system would write such an awful letter. I recognize that they were probably trying to cover themselves in some legal way, but the cruelty of the letter and it's obvious intent to intimidate and scare me was unacceptable.

I am just glad that Brian had enough faith and confidence to help me forget about the letter. Later on, we showed it to Kathy and she said the same thing Brian did. She was very disappointed in the system just like we were.

We were married on July 22, 2011 in the Draper Utah Temple, one of the temples of our church. Brian is always teasing me about being late. I was late even to my own wedding. I had to stop and get something to eat. I was really hungry. Later he told me that he was scared and thought that I had changed my mind.

In the temple, we knelt across the altar from each other and we were sealed for time and all eternity. Looking into his eyes as the ordinance was done, I still wondered if this was all a dream. Could something this good really happen to me? Nothing good ever happened to me. This had to be a dream. It was not.

CHAPTER 21

Our First Child

AFTER THE HONEYMOON, WE MOVED into the basement apartment of Brian's parents' house. The 860 square feet might seem small to some, but it was more space than I had ever had, and twice as much space as I shared with nine people back home in Africa.

To us, it was paradise. I cooked and he worked and cleaned (I understandably hate cleaning). We were both on cloud nine. We had bills piling up that we could not afford from our immigration attorney. We also had hospital bills from my frequent emergency room visits, but we were so happy.

We both wanted to have a baby right away. We just felt like it is what God wanted us to do. Barely a month after we were married, I started feeling sick and began taking pregnancy tests. I wanted to know so badly if I was pregnant. I just kept on taking test after test, sometimes up to two in one day. About two months after our wedding, Brian told me to wait a couple of weeks and then try and take another one.

Three days later, I went into the bathroom and took a new test. I could not believe my eyes! I saw a little plus sign and I started to cry. I told Brian to come into the bathroom. He looked at it and smiled really big and gave me a long hug. We both cried for a long time.

It was one of my most precious memories, standing there hugging each other, crying because we were so happy that our family was starting. Our little baby was on the way.

For some reason we both knew he was a boy, so we decided to name him Michael after our friend that set us up. We started buying baby clothes and getting ready for a boy. We just knew it was a boy.

I was sick for the entire nine months. I was so miserable about how I felt, but so happy to see how tenderly Brian took care of me. I never knew a man like him existed. He did everything so that I did not have to.

When I was about 37 weeks pregnant, I started having really painful contractions. More painful than any other ones that I had had. We called Brian's sister over, who was acting as my doula, and I told her what was going on. She said that it sounded like I was in labor and so she started coaching me through it.

After about 18 hours, the contractions finally started getting more frequent and I was starting to dilate. We went to the hospital. When I got there they put me in a room and put a monitor on my stomach to measure my contractions.

For some inexplicable reason, my contractions had slowed way down. They checked me to see if I was dilated and somehow it had gone back to normal. They sent me home and told me it was just normal contractions.

Right when I got home, my contractions started getting really strong again. I was shocked when Eva checked me again, and said "it looks like you are about two centimeters dilated again. We went back to the hospital again and again the same thing happened.

They sent me home, and said, "These are normal." They said I needed to wait to come back in until they got more extreme. It was pretty obvious that they did not believe me when I told them how extreme the contractions had been.

We realized that I was getting too nervous at the hospital because they kept on interrupting my breathing by checking my monitors. I was too nervous about what they were doing and I could not focus on having the baby.

The real problem was they would not let me stay long enough to get comfortable. They had a limit on how long they would let you stay before your water broke.

Finally after we were sent home for the second time, my water broke. We then went back into the hospital and were able to give them proof that my water had broken. They finally allowed me to stay. They gave me an epidural and I fell asleep and was finally able to relax.

About 15 minutes later, my favorite midwife, Jennifer Krebbs, came in and woke me up.

"You are dilated to eight centimeters," she said. "Are you ready to have a baby?"

I only had to push for about two minutes and Michael was born. 56 hours of labor and he was finally here. Jennifer immediately laid him on my chest. I could not believe what had just happened. I was holding my little Michael.

He lifted up his head and looked at me. They say that babies cannot see this early, but he looked right at me. He could probably just feel that I was there and he knew I was his mother.

I held him there for about ten minutes. Then they took him away for his bath. I looked over at Brian and he was smiling from ear to ear. He leaned over and kissed me on the forehead.

"I am so proud of you," he whispered in my ear.

That night, the nurses kept on wanting to take Michael to the nursery to allow me to get some sleep. However, I just could not sleep without him there. So I kept on calling them to have them bring him in and lay him on my chest. Brian could not sleep when Michael was in there because he was afraid that he would roll off of my chest and fall on the ground.

So my loving husband agreed he would stay up all night and watch me to make sure that the baby did not fall so that I could get some sleep. Holding him and knowing that he was safe in my arms was the only way I could relax. We were both so exhausted. I was so grateful for Brian and that he was willing to do that for me.

We could not qualify for insurance, so after the baby was born there was a tidal wave of bills. They added to our other bills we accumulated for our frequent trips to the emergency room I had throughout the pregnancy. I felt so guilty for running up so much debt with the hospital.

One day when we got a new batch of bills. I looked them over and saw that they totaled over $4,000 just from that day. I was so sad I was causing all of our money problems. When Brian came home, I showed him the bills. He looked over them one at a time

"Eh...who cares?" he said as he shrugged his shoulders. He then gave me a big hug and a kiss. What would I do without his carefree personality? "God will take care of us," he said as he put in the next episode of our favorite TV show *Monk* and sat on the couch.

On another occasion, we were at home when I started getting the same excruciating pain in my stomach that I had been to the Emergency room for so many times before.

"Do you want to go to the emergency room?" Brian asked.

"I am putting us into so much debt," I said. "Let's just let whatever is going to happen, happen. If I die then I die," I said.

"Do not ever worry about money when it comes to your safety. I would rather be a million dollars in debt than have anything happen to you that we could have prevented," he said.

I still felt bad, but knowing that he cared about me more than money made everything okay.

Since then, God has blessed Brian with a better job, and through countless miracles we have been able to pay off all of our hospital debt. Thanks to the efforts of our amazing immigration attorney Lynn McMurray, I have been granted permanent residency. God has also given us a little girl. We named her Tayla. She is now 18 months old and so adorable.

I cannot begin to express how happy I now am. I do not know what I did, but I am glad/grateful God has decided to give me such a beautiful life. I do know that I am going to make the most of it.

I hope that whoever you are and wherever you are reading my story, that it helps you see that God has a plan for you. In my darkest moments, sometimes I wondered if He had forgotten me or if I had done something to deserve what was happening. But I know now that He was there with me through it all, and He is with you too.

About the Author

BORN IN SIERRA LEONE, CHRISTIANA Crawley survived civil war as a young child only to wind up in the United States foster care system after she was abused by the people who brought her to America.

Thanks to the goodness of God, Christiana went on to attend Salt Lake Community College; met her husband, Brian; and had two children.

Her story was featured in *The Salt Lake Tribune* in 2010.